The Asian Women Writers' Workshop is a London-based group that was established in 1984.

Its aim is to reduce the isolation of Asian women writing with few cultural precedents. All the work in this anthology has been developed through a workshop process, whereby each piece has been discussed and read by all members. The Workshop welcomes new writers who would like to work in this type of forum. Most of the writers have not been previously published. This anthology is the first of its kind to be published in Britain.

RIGHT OF WAY

*PROSE AND POETRY
BY THE ASIAN WOMEN
WRITERS' WORKSHOP*

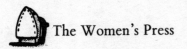 The Women's Press

First published by The Women's Press Ltd 1988
A member of the Namara Group
34 Great Sutton Street, London EC1V ODX

'Right of Way' is an extract from Leena Dhingra's novel *Amritvela*
(The Women's Press, 1988). 'Leaving Home' by Rahila Gupta first appeared in
Imprint magazine, Bombay, February 1988.

British Library Cataloguing in Publication Data
Asian Women Writers' Workshop
    Right of way.
    1. Oriental literature (English)——
    Women authors   2. Oriental literature
    (English)——20th century
    I. Title
    820.8′099287   PR9415

    ISBN 0-7043-4091-7

Typeset by AKM Associates (UK) Ltd,
Ajmal House, Hayes Road, Southall, Middx.
Printed and bound in Great Britain by
Cox and Wyman, Reading, Berks.

Contents

Introduction

When we set out to get an anthology of our work published, most of us had never been published before. Even fewer of us had set aside time to devote exclusively to writing, so we were only able to write in what we believed to be inspired bursts of energy. Thus, an anthology seemed to be well suited to us and it also seemed the best way to represent all the talent in the workshop.

The workshop was formed in 1984, originally the result of lone efforts by Ravi Randhawa, who had managed to get the support of Black Ink and funding from the Greater London Council. Now we are getting financial support from Greater London Arts and Lambeth Council. The workshop was the first of its kind for Asian women writers in Britain, and was meant to draw out any isolated woman who wanted to write but needed a supportive environment to achieve this. The need for this kind of group was poignantly expressed in one of our early meetings when a younger woman, born in Britain, confronted an older woman who had just finished reading a moving story with the question, 'Where were you when I was growing up?' Did it take that long for 'immigrants' to feel settled and strong enough to want to express, re-order and interpret their reality for themselves and society at large? We were also working in a vacuum; there seemed to be no precedents to which we could refer. A few Asian women had been published, but not enough to set up parameters which we could break or work within. Organising as a group gave us visibility, credibility and access to institutions, publishers, and other groups in the community. The workshop gave us the confidence to approach publishers, which as individuals we might never have done. It answered the vital question that haunted all of us: is my writing of any interest or use to anyone else?

In its short history, many women came and went but now a core group of around ten women appears to have crystallised. Although this provides continuity, it also leads to complacency, as most of us are familiar with each other's work, politics and style of criticism. It also works against our original purpose, that of attracting and supporting new talent. Perhaps the stability of this core group is itself intimidating to newcomers and we are constantly discussing and implementing new ways of being more welcoming.

Most of us have found the workshop process useful. It is a stimulus to write when all other methods of self-discipline have failed. You know that, within a few weeks, the other members will be looking askance at you if you have not brought any reading to the workshop. It must be said that many of us are in full-time employment and almost all of us have families to contend with, which means that time devoted to writing has to be negotiated. As this is not a paying proposition, our bargaining power is considerably weakened.

Suggestions and criticism provide new perspectives, new directions for work which might have dried up in your mind. What critical standards we are, and should be, using, are questions that have led to heated but unresolved debates. We tend to use personal statements to reduce the edge of criticism, so that a writer's work is not subjected to some implicit, universal, objective criteria (such as poetry having to have complex imagery). We have to ask who formulated these criteria, and are they relevant to us, as Asian women writing in a country where writers are recognised as great on the terms of white middle-class male critics. How do we evolve our own standards without falling into the other trap of venerating every word written by Black women purely because their disadvantaged position has reduced them to silence?

Though we see ourselves as British-based Asian women, not all of us were bred and born here, and we brought with us different cultural and literary influences. This affected our critical responses. Some of us found it difficult to appreciate translations of Urdu or

2

Bengali poetry. Anglicised responses to the style being flowery or sentimental demanded discussion and contextualisation. Short stories which were rooted in the literary traditions of the sub-continent were considered to have abrupt endings; further discussion revealed that the marked ambiguity of the endings was common to our literary traditions. Criticisms of work seemed to be much easier on political grounds. Positions were clearly drawn and we were able to say about the content, for example, this is classist, patronising, communalist, heterosexist, or whatever. But how did we respond to work where there were no political disagreements but where, for instance, a poem simply failed to move you? As a group we have yet to define our literary criteria. If you say of a poem that it is full of 'bald and simplistic' statements, that should be 'woven through images', can you be sure that this is not merely your own conditioned response to 'good' and 'bad' styles of writing?

This does not mean that there was always a consensus of political views. When we made the transition from a workshop to a collective, political arguments arose from the name we should give ourselves. Some of us suggested that we should call ourselves 'black' women to show our alignment with that part of the movement which believes that Asian and Afro-Caribbean women face a common oppression and that the way ahead is to fight together. Others felt that they had been squeezed out of black women's writing groups where the women were predominantly Afro-Caribbean and the implicit attitude was that the term 'black' belonged to them. Yet others felt that there were cultural differences which would make it difficult to respond critically and knowledgeably to Afro-Caribbean writing and vice versa. There was also the feeling that there was no Asian women's forum and that in order to encourage young women writing for the first time to join, our composition should be reflected in our name. Consensus was reached when it was said that we should work closely with black women's groups and participate in all events for black women writers.

The second big debate was sparked off by the word 'women' in the name. Were we not feminists, should it not be Asian feminist writers? Many women felt that the word feminist had been sullied by the exclusiveness and racism of white middle-class women and, therefore, was no longer a useful term for us. There were such differences in our understanding of feminism that in any case the term would have been completely meaningless as a way of selecting new women to become members of the workshop. Also, it would have meant overturning the original idea of the workshop, which pre-dated many of us: the forum should be available to all Asian women. That these issues were not resolved was frustrating but also led to interesting debates in which work was viewed in a political context and the relationship between writing and politics became clearer. The very fact that we needed to set up a group for a particular section of society was an enunciation of the political realities that normally excluded women like us. Consciousness developed through the workshop process of our need to write in a particular way, to take into account our own class position when writing and to recognise the way in which this distorted our perceptions, and of our need for positive but realistic images of Asian women.

More recently, we found that the open door policy had to be changed. It was simply unworkable. We spent hours arguing about the communalist and classist sentiments in the work of some members. Consciousness raising was futile when the gap was so unbridgeable. Anti-lesbian views were sometimes expressed. A resolution was passed that we as a group were opposed to racist, communalist, classist and anti-lesbian attitudes and writings so that there was some communality, some given assumptions, upon which we could build further.

Unfortunately, the anthology took up so much energy that some of the new women who joined after the manuscripts were submitted found it difficult to relate to a group which was so preoccupied with its own tail – its own finished product. Then we started to revive an earlier attempt to select work for a 'readings' collection, so that we had a ready pool of material to take with us when invited to do readings by other groups. This provided an impetus to write as well. However, the impetus was not strong enough. We have now started negotiations with newspapers and magazines to serialise a selection of new writing so as to stimulate work. We also invited women writers to talk about their work or to run workshops. Amongst ourselves we rotated the running of workshops where we set each other exercises. We found this very useful. It shattered all our romantic notions about writing only when inspired. It showed us that if we worked at something, even when we were exhausted after our day's work, we could come up with a fairly readable piece. It also redefined writing so that we saw it as a craft, a tool which could be honed and perfected with effort; it chased away any elitist notions of being born with a talent. In a world where literacy skills are limited, we were forced to recognise the privilege of our positions.

Most of our writing had been shared mainly by public readings, and this affected our style of writing. We felt that we had to be short, punchy, direct, rhetorical and dramatic. As our method of operation in the workshop was also reading our material aloud to each other and then discussing it, we never looked at our writing from the point of view of the written page, where it is possible to hold the attention of the reader with more complex structures. What was boring when read aloud for thirty minutes looked quite different when read privately. This became important when we launched the idea of an anthology: we had to see pieces not merely in terms of performance.

Preparation for the anthology also changed the aims and objectives of the workshop. We started to look at it as a launching pad for our own careers as writers. Practical problems had to be dealt with, such as finding agents, obtaining commissions, understanding publishing contracts, making contacts, gaining membership of writers' unions, approaching employers for fees, presentation of work. This narrower focus eclipsed our aim of developing writing in the community, of doing outreach work with Asian women in a wider context. This needs to be revived and developed. Perhaps this will come with our next phase.

The collective is open to new members who meet the criteria mentioned above and who present a piece of writing within six months of joining. Being London based, it excludes women living elsewhere, who may be even more isolated, but this is something we want to try to overcome. We could share the skills we have picked up over the last few years with women who want to start groups in other parts of the country. Some of us are willing to travel to help in any way we can.

Pedal Push

'Man Beware! Woman Gonna Get Your Sanity.'

She should come one evening and rub it off.

As it was it pricked her mood to defiance and perhaps that's why she never did. Inevitably the lights would be on red, and as she and her bike came to a squealing stop, her eyes would seek their morning communion with the writing on the wall; and as the lights changed she'd carry it away like a frame for the day, stirring it into Colin's coffee as he rushed into the office and unwound from the morning's family feuding.

Today's argument had been about who was going to run the children to school and how he couldn't see why his wife couldn't do it. After all, as far as he could see she didn't have much work to do, with all the mod cons and labour-saving devices he'd bought her, not to mention Mrs Daily the cleaner, who acted more like his wife's counsellor than a cleaner; he supposed it was co-counselling, because his wife was hardly the one to sit quiet while there was talking to be done.

She listened and watered the plants and picked up the letters and in between sips and grievances his eyes ran their daily course over her body. She was dressed in a shalwar/kameez with a shimmering dupatta sliding over her shoulders; Colin liked a bit of exotica in his office.

'I've applied for that law course. Will you write me a reference?' she asked, settling in behind her desk and starting to rip open the morning's mail, much as she imagined his wife relished ripping into him. 'I like your wife,' she added for cold comfort.

Colin moaned as if in pain. 'What will I do?'

7

She supposed his cup was empty. 'Oh, you'll have lots of fun choosing a replacement,' lifting the coffee flask from near his elbow and refilling his cup.

Telephone calls, clients, typing: the mosaic of the morning's work filtered the time through to munchtime/lunchtime and Colin came out, having combed his hair and adjusting his tie. 'Switch the answering slave on. I'm meeting Paul at the wine bar. Want to come?' She shook her head and he smiled a knowing smile. 'The intellectual boyfriend?'

Pradeep was sitting near the back and didn't see her as she came in. She was always struck by a pang of disappointment when she saw him, his well-dressed executive appearance the very opposite of her romantic cravings for a book-carrying, scraggy-haired revolutionary who was going to sort out the world. Cliché! She knew; continuing, however, to nurture the hope that life would not prove to be as ordinary as it threatened to be. What was her mind up to? Disloyalty! Guilt-tripping over this brush with treachery, her hello smile oozed more than her feelings were prepared to give. His eyes lit up as he said how nice she looked, and, as his compliment acted like an erasure over her lips, he handed her the menu. 'I've ordered.'

Pradeep asked why she didn't marry him; he would finish his Ph.D. at the end of the year and was sure to get a good job. An American University had already approached him. Wouldn't she like to leave this place and go and live in the sun somewhere? She could carry on with her law studies if she really wanted to, but in a few years they would have to think of children.

No. No. Marriage was frightening. She had hardly yet tasted freedom.

'But there is no freedom,' he said, 'only choices, and with time choices, don't expand, only contract. Take me to see your parents. They will like me.' She knew they would and that was why for so long she had kept him so far away. He was a secret, for they would not approve of their daughter adopting a boyfriend; immodest and brazen behaviour! Unsuitable for their quiet, well-respected family. But if Pradeep went as the-man-who-wished-to-marry-her they would welcome him and forgive her. For he was all that

8

they would want and all that they would look for if they themselves were looking, which of course they were, except that they would not have aspired as high as a Ph.D. Their daughter was only a secretary, and arranged marriages must perforce take account of economic and academic compatibility.

'Bye' she said, fingers licking up the last of the apple pie. 'Can't be late.'

Got the rest of my life to live, can't let it come to a dead stop in the Pizza Hut, can I? Almost slipping over a banana skin as she stepped out.

Getting back to the office and wondering how many times she would have to come back before she could change circumstances and move on; half seeing a tall man straighten up as she approached, his outdated afro shivering in the cold.

'I thought this was an English practice,' following her into the office.

'Black coffee?' tones contemptuous.

'Not that you lot want much to do with any of us, anyhow.'

'Our lot,' tones statistical, 'get attacked more often than your lot, and your lot join up with them lot . . .'

'What's going on? A tribal war?' Colin, standing full and replete in the doorway.

They were both embarrassed into silence, that one word reducing them to their old colonial status.

'How can you work for him?' he asked as Colin disappeared into the office.

'How can you hire him as your solicitor?'

'Necessity is the mother of compromise.'

When he came out of Colin's office it was a 'see you Bombay, Baby' and a quick exit out the door before she could retaliate.

Days come and go, the seasons drift by, the files in the office turn round like revolving doors. She thinks one name is the same as another and all the cases merge into a blur of broken homes, broken limbs and a sordid saga of 'not me, it was him/her/they who dunnit,' till she felt like she was working in life's casualty ward. Colin told her she was romanticising, wait till she got married, then she'd really find out what it was all about; she should count herself lucky she was having a dress rehearsal; and could she book tickets because wifey wanted to go and see some play, and if she herself was so inclined, to book herself one, too, the more the merrier, especially when wifey was around; and while she was at it why not get one for the cleaner; and it was only her look of exasperation that brought to a halt his plans for a drama of revenge.

Threats, not revenge, slithered through Pradeep's conversations: casually recounted anecdotes of the many who had loved, lost and lived to regret. Hints of the many who would be interested in as good a match as him, socio-eulogising on the system of arranged marriage and how parents more often than not managed to hit the mark, and wasn't it strange about the English? Strange for a culture that purported not to believe in fate, to rely on that old hack Cupid, who never had learnt to shoot straight, to provide them with their nearest and dearest . . . She felt as if a doctor was writing her a prescription and telling her she should be a good girl and swallow the medicine and everything would be all right.

'It's not nice to be alone in a world of copulating couples,' said someone in the supermarket queue, and she thought, so true, but could she, should she, even if she wanted to. Though her mother would say that obstinacy is a one-way road.

Her parents were talking about the future and their old age. They would go back to India, they were saying; it was the only place for the aged. They would sit out in the sun, letting the heat soak into their old bones, hire a servant to look after them, and spend the day in gossip and chit-chat; at ease at last, their right to be and belong unquestioned. She listened, and thought about herself and panicked. What would she do when she was old? Could she go back? But she'd never had a life there. No one knew her. She would be a stranger all over again, more of a stranger than here. What were they going to do? All the black people who were young like her but who would soon be old like their parents?

Tomas and his afro came in on Tuesday, right after Colin, early for his appointment, cutting short Colin's list of the morning's domestic disasters. Colin picked up his coffee and took his disgruntlement into his office. Tomas leaned over and placed two

10

tickets on her desk. 'Bring your bloke along.' How did he know? How many others knew? 'And will you come to my trial in one of your sparkly scarves? I'll be able to look at its lights in that boring courtroom.'

Colin said that Tomas would probably get a sentence, and though he didn't personally believe in stereotypes, as far as he could see Tomas was as stereotyped as anyone could get. She hadn't wanted to go to Tomas' gig but now she did and it meant a fight at home. They couldn't understand why she wanted to go off to this Black music thing; she knew it wasn't so much the music as the Black and she thought, something's got to change somewhere, and because Colin's forecast had scratched a foreboding into her mind, she wore one of her sparkliest saris and when she met Pradeep at the tube he wanted to know why she was so dressed up.

Tomas saw her in the glimmering dimness and, leaving the stage, came over to give her a kiss and asked was it bad at home and she replied yes and added, this was no better, ears droopy with disappointment. He promised to get her tickets for a programme of *ghazals* and self-smiling at this rip in his image returned to join the band.

The bike had a puncture on the way into work one day and when she arrived, wet, cold and miserable, Colin made her coffee and brought in a take-away lunch and she thought how nice he was, till his wife rang up and said did he only make lunch appointments with her so's he could forget them and Colin said, I haven't told you what happened this morning and she said she had a headache and could she go home early. He ordered a taxi but he didn't like not having an audience and she promised to advertise for a replacement the next day.

Tomas got six months and said it don't matter he'd get some reading done and she promised to visit him and he declined because it would cause ructions at her home. Don't matter, she thought, too, it ain't the end of the world, and who can say who's a stereotype? 'I threatened to immolate myself on the altar of their prejudice.' Pradeep's mouth froze open, kebab arrested half-way between plate and palate.

'How?'

She picked up a lettuce leaf and tearing it into shreds told him how she'd announced that she was going to get her hair braided and beaded. 'Mother said, "That'll be nice, the tribals in India do their hair like that." I felt like a squashed tomato.' He couldn't understand why it was so important to her. He sounded peeved. Engrossed in her explanation, she didn't notice. 'Because it's racism, isn't it? No point in beating about the bush, is there? There's not much morality on our side if we do it and yet criticise the whites for doing it, too.' His mouth had closed but she could see it opening again, not to eat but to interrupt. He didn't get a chance. 'I know it's complicated and not as simple as I've just made it out to be, and I know about the brainwashing from colonialism. But no one else can change us. We've got to do it, ourselves. It's no good giving people lectures. Practice and example, that's what's needed. That's why they've got to come round to being friends with Tomas.'

'Very commendable.' He left without making the usual arrangements for their next rendezvous.

Two months of perpetual pestering shifted the gears of her mother's prejudice, activating a samosa-making session, ready for when they'd visit together, and she laughed at this application of her mother's old family rule and ruse: 'If you can't talk to them – feed them.'

Colin's wife came to the office and said she'd seen the advertisement and couldn't she apply for the job? She sat right down and filled in an application form and then they both went out to lunch and Colin's wife said, 'I hope this isn't going to be seen as canvassing, though of course I'm sure the interviewing panel will be above suspicion.'

The next day Colin nearly choked on his coffee, just when he happened to be leafing through the application forms, and she had to thump him and thump him before he recovered, though all red in the face, with tears running down his cheeks. 'Why don't you postpone your studies for a year?' he said. 'You'll gain invaluable experience and be top of the class when you start the course.'

'I'll take those,' leaning forward and extracting the mangled

12

papers from his clutch. 'Some good candidates, don't you think? Have more coffee.'

Pradeep was pulling on her mind for a decision, and she said, 'I'm busy buying books. Come along and help me choose.'

'No can do,' he said, 'I'm off to the States.' She complained, justifiably she thought, that she'd just started her course and he smiled and replied that that was okay, he wasn't about to ask her to go with him.

'Oh,' she said. 'I think I need some sugar in my coffee,' reaching over for the bowl and like in silent slow-motion seeing it slip in between her fingers, releasing an avalanche of sugar over the table and on to the floor.

It took longer to cycle to college, but the exercise helped the pain in her heart. Why didn't you go with him, asked the wheels each day as they turned around, he was only waiting for you to say so. 'He could have waited for me anyhow,' pumping the wheels harder to drown their chatter, but they came straight back and said, he asked you, didn't he, couldn't do no more. 'He only asked for what he wanted. Everything had to be his way. He could have waited till I'd finished.' The wheels lifted over a bump and flinging her forward told her he'd really cared, over the years, and if she'd cared she would've gone, wouldn't she? Wouldn't she?

'If he'd cared, he would've stayed. Nothing wrong with going fifty-fifty. I couldn't do it all his way. Do it once and you'll do it always. I wish this damn pain would go away.' The nights were getting dark early now and one night she bought a pot of paint and a brush and did some editing on the writing on the wall:

'Woman Beware! Man Gonna Get Your Sanity.'

Ravinder Randhawa

13

The Breasts that Spout

The Breasts are furious.
I took them on trains and buses
Through stations, lavatories, schools and offices,
Up to Leicester and through Manchester
On a will of iron, hard like a stone,
Away from the mouth
That parts to house them.

I was seeking a solution
And fleeing Motherhood,
Like a bus-stop to be unheeded.
Now my breasts leak persistently,
Dampen my blouse revengefully,
Cry blue-white tears to nurture posterity.
I must decide.

Head strong, heart yearning,
Bra wet, breast burning.
Breasts compelling, brown shields,
Spreading their heat a soothing balm.
I'll travel down and accept the call,
Like scaffolding out on hire
Kiss the tiny hands and feet
Through the grille of caring.

In fleeing, in returning,
In building, in loving,
Moulding a new destiny.
So unbutton the blouse
And direct the path of
The unruly ones –
The breasts that spout.

Kanta Talukdar

Guerrilla Warfare

Bulkimashi was known to be kind and good-natured, never bearing anyone any umbrage. She possessed an inner strength which made her oblivious to the vagaries of her companions and helped her cull sobriety and tolerance from the frequent muddles that were inflicted upon her. I remember the time her husband, Kanumama, a fiercely upright little man of seventy, came walking into our house on a very hot summer's day. Miniature puddles of sweat kept dripping off him as he asked for four glasses of water. Kanumama had always been a bit of an eccentric and his request for four glasses of water was taken at face value, just like the whiskers on his ears, which he had recently taken to plaiting.

Drinking up two glasses of water, he ostentatiously pushed the other two to his left-hand side and said, 'Come on, drink it up,' to no one in particular. Kanumama was the eldest in the family. His was a position of special respect. One was not allowed to smoke or drink alcohol in front of him, leave alone ask him questions like, 'Who are you talking to, Kanumama?'

As my parents were out, my brother and I did our best to entertain him. My brother brought out his collection of worms while I tried to restrain our fox terrier whose bark had on an earlier occasion driven Kanumama on to the dining-table.

For about half an hour we carried on chatting to Kanumama, intermittently nonplussed by some of his comments which seemed to be directed to the space on his left side. All of a sudden he bellowed, 'Drink it up, stupid woman, you'll get heatstroke otherwise.' As there was no other woman in the room I stretched my hand out towards the glasses, inwardly outraged, but at that my uncle bellowed even louder, 'Not you, stupid girl, I mean your silly aunt.'

But my aunt, birdlike and frail Bulkimashi, hadn't come with him. Registering the astonishment on our faces, Kanumama turned to his left side. 'But I left the house with her,' he stuttered weakly. 'We even had a long conversation on the bus.' Slipping on his shoes and brushing down the folds of his dhoti, he trotted briskly down the stairs.

My brother and I weren't too surprised. Misunderstandings kept supervening Kanumama and Bulkimashi's fifty-year-old marriage. Tacitly it was agreed among the family that 'the rough diamond' that Kanumama was had not been the best choice for the suave and highly educated Bulkimashi. But her father had insisted . . . Their marriage was like a wrinkled up cardboard box, which intermittently opened up at the seams, letting its contents proclaim their separate existence, despite prolonged association.

My brother and I dashed to the balcony to wave Kanumama a hurried goodbye. Just then we saw Bulkimashi walking serenely through the wrought iron gates. There were jasmine blossoms in her hair and not a fold out of place in her freshly starched white sari. Kanumama almost knocked her down in his hurry.

Coming to our house Kanumama had jumped on to a bus, not looking back to see whether Bulkimashi had caught it, too. He had carried on chatting to her throughout the journey, right up to our house, not waiting for a reply, an old habit of his. The Bengali custom of the wife walking several steps behind the husband compounded the confusion.

We never found out whether Bulkimashi had missed the bus deliberately or not.

Kanta Talukdar

16

The Law of the Market-Place

In the back street
of the capital city
stalls and shops stretch out
on to the pavement.
Passers-by stop to examine
crates, baskets, sacks
and jars
filled with colour and abundance.

Fragrant rice
and freshwater fish
from Bangladesh,
cloves and cinnamon sticks
from Tangiers,
marrows and chillies
from East Africa stimulate
the palates of the rich and the exiled.

Surprise and curiosity for some –
nostalgia for others
who've left behind
a piece of land
where golden hopes were planted.

They till the land
and harvest the crops
but don't taste them.
They pack them, load them on to
ships to the West.
Arms, ammunition, come back in return.

Sibani Raychaudhuri

Careers

At five they want to be
Spaceman, Princess,
Superwoman.

They dream of
the A-team, ET,
and Knight Rider's computerised car.

At eight they want to be
fireman, dustman, postman,
nurse – the people
whose work has built their world.

By thirteen, the word 'Ambition'
shines brightly but remote –
they cannot reach,
and how to get there
they do not know.

At sixteen
a cold wind blows
along the long corridors
across the concrete spaces –
no jobs for them.
They stand in line
to sign on.

Sibani Raychaudhuri

The Nightmare

'What's your name, dear?' Fariha heard the nurse's voice dimly. The question irked her consciousness pushing through veils of numbness which swathed her head. She thought worryingly that the answer would surface if only, if only she had a moment to remember.

'Farr-ee, Farr-ee,' she suddenly heard her brother's childish voice as they trudged through the muddy swamp, netting tadpoles with their mother's dupatta.

'Oh, Furro! Really! How many times have I told you people that these are not fish, they're tadpoles? Disgusting. Now go and wash your hands and face before your father comes in.'

But he was right behind them, fuming as he walked in. 'Her name is not Furro. Why must you people insist on calling her Furro and Farree? She's got a perfectly simple and beautiful name, Fariha. Now don't let me catch anyone calling her anything else but by her proper name. Her name is Fariha.'

Fariha felt a little puzzled as she looked up. Her father wasn't there any more. It was her husband Salim who was saying those words. 'I like to call her Fairy, though, that was my special name for her.'

'Doesn't she speak any English?' the nurse asked, looking at her pityingly as if that in fact was the worst ailment that could befall anyone.

Fariha started to sing in a low voice,

'Sing mother sing,
Mother can sing,
Mother sing to Pat
Pat sing to mother . . .'

She could still recall the face of her English teacher quite clearly, Colonel Mahmud's wife Margaret, her blonde hair dulled by the sun and her fair skin always looking a tortured red in the blazing heat of the summer. Everybody said how utterly unsuited they were. The servants had seen them sling plates at each other at dinner time.

'These English women don't know how to get along with their husbands,' her mother used to say. 'Marriages don't work without an effort. You have to work at them. A man is like a vessel, hard and unchanging, and a good woman should be like water, flow and adapt herself to his shape.'

She looked up at Salim's face. Hard and unchanging; he was hard. And then when his body hardens and pushes flapping against cold thighs, demanding to be contained, she must yield . . . She wondered about being a vessel herself sometimes. Would she break if she didn't yield? Must she yield even when her whole being revolted against each slithery panting thrust? They told me nothing about that, she thought angrily. But it must be all right. Not like that other time when old, dry exploring fingers chafed against her body, hurting her deep inside, accompanied by Uncle Jamal's rasping voice whispering, 'This is our little secret, little one, don't tell anyone. No one will understand.' She worried. What if anyone should find out about it? It seemed all wrong and dirty.

And then, Salim. Not saying much, ever, urgent, businesslike. Everyone must do it that way if that was the way to get babies. And the babies were lined up in tall vessels all along the top shelf of the path. lab. when they went for a blood test after she'd recovered from typhoid that year when almost everyone got typhoid. Tall glass jars full of clear fluid containing grotesquely malformed foetuses. Fazlu, the driver, had told her what they were.

'I suppose she's been depressed really since last April, when she had to have this abortion. She'd really wanted the baby, you see. I didn't realise then how much. But we had to go in for a termination because Sunny, our youngest, got German measles. The test, I mean the amniocentesis, indicated some abnormality but she wouldn't believe the doctors. Kept insisting that the baby would be okay. I had to be firm. There was no choice.'

Salim's face wore an expression of sanctimonious concern mixed with apology for his wife's foolishness.

'And what is the matter with your right shoulder, dear?' the nurse asked Fariha after filling in the admission forms.

'It hurts, really hurts. But don't look at it, it's nasty to look at. It's where the bird got me, a nasty deep wound. That sharp beak, it was hard, so hard. It plunged deeper each time. Drew blood, I couldn't move, couldn't do anything.' Fariha was becoming shrill and excited.

'There's nothing there, darling,' Salim intervened, stroking her shoulder gently, but to his embarrassment Fariha cowered reflexively.

'Oh? What bird was this then?' Cool blue eyes sought Salim's glance.

'Well, you see,' Salim began, 'Fairy had this awful nightmare. Didn't you, darling? It was only a nightmare, wasn't it?'

Fariha responded to the sharpness of his tone with a dull nod. 'Yes, yes,' she mumbled, suddenly calmer. 'A nightmare, only a nightmare.'

Salim jerked his head towards Fariha and began in an ironic tone. 'All this business began with this awful nightmare.' He felt uncomfortable at being questioned. The nurse must think he'd been battering her. 'A nightmare about two birds, a huge, vicious-looking vulture and a trembly little dove. The vulture kept pecking with his sharp beak into the dove's wing and the dove wouldn't move, couldn't get away. It just stood there mesmerised, allowing itself to be tortured. Ghastly nightmare, she never told me then. Told Pinky, my daughter, I mean, our daughter, about it.

'Then the nightmare kept recurring. Sometimes she'd be too frightened to sleep. Now she's so confused she thinks she's the dove. There isn't the slightest mark on her shoulder though, you can see for yourself.'

Staff Nurse Smithers smiled to reassure him. 'I understand.'

Salim sighed, feeling a little vindicated. 'It hasn't been easy, Nurse. Come home after a long day to a place that's a pigsty and nothing to eat in the kitchen. It's been hard on the kids. Just accusations and tears, and hallucinations and tears and tears . . .

'I'm an honest and hard-working man. I worked my way up with my own two hands. It's not been easy. It was a struggle all the way.'

The nurse nodded sympathetically. Fariha sat as if in a trance. Salim wondered resentfully about her pathetic conduct. And now all this nonsense. Manchester in the sixties hadn't been exactly welcoming towards the crowds of cheap labourers who'd arrived fresh from the sub-continent. Lost amongst those hordes of rustics from the north, struggling to survive, desperately searching for success, and missing them all the time, missing Fairy and missing the children, missing the comforts of home for ten solitary years. And now look at her, what an old bag she's become. It was a shock when he saw them arriving at the airport; talk about the reality betraying the dream. She looked . . . 'fat' . . . his mind had hesitated over the word then. And so much older than she ought. And the children, too. They looked so dark and, for some reason, poverty-stricken. Much darker than he remembered. Yes, the sun bakes you, he reminded himself. They were toddlers when he'd left them. They must go to school now. Funny, he'd always thought they were all three quite fair. Sadly, he realised, in England they'd all be inescapably brown.

He'd consoled himself with the thought that Fairy could look quite nice if she cut her hair, lost some weight and got some decent clothes. He couldn't wait to get started on a programme of therapy for her. Operation Salvage. All the things she had to learn and all that she had to unlearn. Kids had been no problem from the word go. Picked up English really fast, loved the telly, really liked their school, learnt to work the gadgets in the house. But she'd been quite impossible. Depressed and apathetic, so slow, always so slow. He'd never realised before how dull she was, and clumsy.

The nurse was trying to talk to Fariha. 'Would you like to say goodbye to your husband now, dear?'

Fariha looked at her blankly. 'My husband is in England.' Then

22

her voice dropped to a whisper. 'He adores me. I get these blue airmail letters from him regularly. And money, he sends me money. Sometimes the money order can take ages and you have to wait and wait.

'But that's not his fault. It's hard for him, too, over there on his own. Life is hard in England. Last year when I sent him my photograph,' she confided shyly, 'he wrote some verses about me. I showed Nikki the letter and she said how lucky I was to have a husband who really loves me.'

Salim felt uncomfortable. 'I must go now. The children will be waiting.' He began to rush in embarrassed confusion, bending to give her a hasty peck on the cheek. Thanked the nurse and turned away, feeling a certain guilt-tinged relief at being able to leave her behind with the competent staff at Shendley. They'd be able to sort her out. Fancy telling the nurse about his letters. 'My husband is in England . . .' Where the hell does she think Shendley is then, if not in England? New Delhi, I suppose. He felt cross and irritated.

Fariha's mind catapulted her from England to Lahore and back with an ease which disconcerted anyone who attempted to converse with her. Alarmed, the good doctors at Shendley decided to launch immediately on a substantial programme of drug therapy which was so overwhelming that she forgot both London and Lahore and the problems she'd had to contend with in both cities, essentially alone, coping and struggling to cope. Forgot the loneliness, the frustrations and the daily humiliations of her ignorance. Forgot where she was, who she was, why she'd been grieving, and for whom.

She slept and slept and slept. Ate and slept. Sometimes Salim and the children came. If they didn't come she didn't remember to miss them. When they came, she barely remembered who they were. The children looked a little afraid and worried and Salim bustled about ineffectually. But she felt no emotion, no anger, no joy, no grief and no pain.

She did tell Salim about the drugs really knocking her out, making her feel dead weak physically. She was constipated and had an awful chesty cough which wouldn't leave her and she felt unable to think. But Salim would dismiss her complaints and tell her she'd be better soon. What could be better than a hospital like Shendley? 'They all know what to do; this is not the mental hospital in Lahore!'

Fariha had no real grip on time. Six months slipped by but to her they sometimes felt like six years and at other times like six days. She would watch the long afternoons disappearing behind the tall green trees surrounding the hospital, wondering how deep their roots were. Dig them up once and they're dead. Driftwood and dead tree trunks lumbered her thoughts. 'Barren, like I've become, unable to produce a normal baby, when I *so* needed one. What's a woman worth if she can't even bear children?' She could hear Ma and Nanny talking about Zohra, whose husband had remarried because she wouldn't get pregnant.

Salim came alone to fetch her the day she was discharged. When she entered the house she felt almost triumphant to think that she still remembered where all the rooms were. The children were still shy of her. She became vaguely aware that Salim himself looked discomfited and very concerned about something.

'I'm all right now,' she said to reassure him.

Salim's unease grew over the next few days. Finally at the weekend he forced himself to confess.

'I have to tell you something, Fairy. It's not going to be easy. I hope you'll take it sensibly. I don't want to make you ill again.'

'I'm all right now,' she said, trying to allay a sudden panic which threatened to rise in her throat. Her hands reached automatically for her handbag, groping till they'd closed on the pink, triangular pills. A little breathless, she looked him in the eye.

'I've been offered a post in America by my company. It's an honour really for an Asian to be offered a plum post like that. I feel I can't really afford to refuse it.'

She thought for a second. 'If we must live abroad it doesn't terribly matter how far from home . . .'

'It's not that. It's just that they won't give you a visa.' Her stomach knotted up. 'You mean I can't come with you? Why?'

'Because of your history of . . . of . . . You being unwell, I mean.'

'So?'

'I wondered, if, I mean, I really thought, it might be better all round if you went back home for a few months, maybe a year. It would do you a world of good. As soon as the doctor says you are well enough, you'll be able to join us.'

'And the children?' She felt close to tears. A vision of 'back home' flashed through her mind. A room in her mother's damp and dark flat, snipping round her own time and activities to fit into the family's schedule, reverting to her life of fifteen years ago.

'Well, the children must come with me. It's important for them educationally. And then you can join us later.'

He averted his eyes. The American Embassy official's words echoed loud and clear in his brain. 'There's very little chance, Mr Khan, I'd say hardly any, of *her* getting permission to enter the USA. They're fairly strict about this.'

He wondered pityingly about what could comfort her.

'They're older now, they'll miss you, but I think they'll manage. We managed on our own for six months after all, didn't we? This can't be any longer.' The dreaded tears and scene did not ensue, to Salim's surprise and great relief.

Fariha said nothing. She just looked absently at the pills and went to fetch herself a glass of water.

She looked puffy-eyed and drained the next morning. Salim asked her if she'd slept all right.

'Hardly at all. I think I need to go back to bed. I think I'll take a pill and try to go to sleep.'

Salim was concentrating on getting the parting in the middle of his hair exactly where he liked it. 'You see, I kept having this nightmare,' Fariha continued, 'a strange and horrible nightmare, about . . .'

'I know, I know,' he interrupted impatiently. 'Same old nightmare I suppose, about the vulture and the poor little trembly dove. What I can't understand is why the hell doesn't this poor little dove fly away?'

Fariha looked worried as she thought about it. 'Maybe she didn't because she didn't know how to. But now, I think she can't, because she's dead.'

Rukhsana Ahmad

25

The Story of my Womb

This was the second time I had entered hospital. Hospital with its subdued choice of colours, not too clinical, nor too heavy on the eye, a cocoon of sleepjarring yet heartwarming hustle-bustle. It was a strange ward, this gynaecology ward with its ironical mix of women – some there for the termination of stirring lives within their wombs and others to stir some life into theirs. Both sets desperate to exchange their circumstances which destiny had jumbled up in her clumsy way. There was a certain emptiness in the eyes of those in for abortion which set them apart from those whose infertility had not yet killed hope.

I thought back to those years when I was eighteen, when an abortion had returned the defiance to my eyes, when the curve of my tummy had not gone beyond a quite plausible paunch, when eating raw papaya had failed to generate the heat that could purge. I had gone to a charitable institution and had life suctioned out of me – that one seedy afternoon, a quick flip through the directory, a helpful friend, a taxi, an excuse for a day's absence, a general anaesthetic, a weak and watery but overjoyed return to life and it was all over. I had visions of my father equipped with an old shotgun and my mother weaving her dramatic fantasy around the villain who meddled with her daughter's innocence, cut short by this one action-packed day. And how much more sophisticated than using knitting kneedles or twigs that broke inside – suggestions from friends fed on Dadima's stories and gratefully rejected in that one magic rational moment which had escaped the panic.

Whatever the vacuum cleaning technique had achieved in the short term, in the long term my insides had been messed up. Years later, after a lot of hesitation and soul-searching, self-righteousness and self-denial, I decided to get pregnant. But found that reality did not simply follow the desire, Hindi films notwithstanding. I had never doubted my abilities, or rather my fertility, as potential mother. No – doubt I did – eight years of escaping without harm was more than a question of luck or an infallible withdrawal technique (I was psychologically allergic to contraception). That charitable Ram Seth Nursing Home had a lot to answer for.

And yet as I had never tested it, I still hoped. So day after inexhaustible night, I tried every angle on the problem – facing the ceiling, the floor, the mirror, the wardrobe, admiring my toe-nails, his toe-nails – day after fertile (?) day. Vaseline, every conceivable kind of gel, immense willpower to face that penetration which by its regularity was becoming increasingly unpleasant. The precious sperm-laden liquid trickled out – often, I stood on my head (yoga does have its advantages) and waited for a minute or two, hoping my posture would facilitate ease of passage. Why didn't anyone tell me about the anti-gravity drive of the sperm? Tried being sperm-logged, stopped playing tennis in case it dislodged my precious load. The house suddenly appeared to be inhabited by phallic wonders, aggravating a persecution complex that hints were falling hard and heavy.

After the middle of every month, I was convinced I'd done it. I'd examine every yawn in the morning for traces of nausea, every sensation of the world spinning for signs of faintness (those damned Hindi films again). And I'd feel set for stagnation and complacency for the next nine months. I'd wait for the first day of factual proof. Each time, the red carpet (an image entrenched in my mind from a sex education class at my convent school) would be wrenched away and flushed out.

And whenever I went home, I saw uncomprehending blank faces – withered and weathered by the village sun, women 'unliberated', giving point to their lives by bearing children endlessly. They looked at me – thirty, married, no children. They could understand inevitability; they could not understand choice. And I chose to confuse them, to 'liberate' them from their unbroken moulds of thought and say, 'out of choice'. Immoral, they would have said, if I

27

was a stranger, but as I was family, they said, she's a modern girl. I preferred that damnation to hints of cursed infertility. Choice took me out of their ranks, placed me above them, let me be contemptuous. The fact of infertility would put me back amongst them. They could cope with that, put me through religious ritual, feed me with birth-inducing foods, initiate symbolic phallus rituals – worship of Shiva's lingam.

Little did they know that, armed with a thermometer, a temperature chart and fertility drugs, I had my own modern rituals. And that one month, on the most auspicious day, a tired going-through-the-motions-with-gritted-teeth affair, ending in a piddly, unworthy, uninspiring trickle of semen, the miraculous happened on earth. And what set in was not complacency but back-breaking fatigue, aching breasts and a phobia of miscarriage. And instead of bringing the happy couple together in a romantic haze of knitted bootees and pattering feet, it brought tensions to the surface. Ranting and raving every day, a storm of tears, walls of incomprehension, hate and despair. Suddenly the realisation – love had vanished, it had been replaced by tolerance years ago, the desire for a child had turned sour, the moment had passed, dead but unmourned.

I didn't want a responsibility that I couldn't share. So here I was in hospital once again – ending what I had longed to start. Bad timing, I thought, I always miss my cue. Meanwhile, love continued to blossom in the plasticity of my cheap novels nurturing ideals which have brought some of us to grief. Many ideals were to die in that one day in hospital. No wonder I found kinship in those empty, wandering confused eyes which refused to talk, which shunned communication – knowing that to start something would foreshadow its end.

Rahila Gupta

The Girl Who Couldn't See Herself

Once upon a time there was a girl who couldn't see herself very clearly, and so she kept stumbling and losing herself all the time. For since she couldn't see herself, she didn't know what she was, or where she fitted in, or how she should behave.

She decided to do something about it and went and bought herself a large mirror and put it up in her room. But when she looked at herself in it, all she saw was a blur. This was most confusing. She turned away from the mirror and sat down to think about it, and then, through the corner of her eye, she caught a reflection of herself in the mirror, but when she turned to see what it was, all that faced her was the same blur. This confused her even more.

She put on her coat, went out and walked down the street, but nobody seemed to notice her. Even in the shop, the cashier simply looked at the goods in the basket, took the note and placed the change on the counter. The girl started to wonder if, maybe, she was invisible, and so, on her way home, she walked right in the middle of the pavement to see what would happen. People gave way to her, some even grumbled as they almost bumped into her, but she returned home feeling reassured that, at least, she wasn't invisible.

'Really, this is most strange,' she thought. 'Why is it that others can see me and I can't see myself?' Then she had an idea. 'Of course,' she said to herself. 'What I'll do is to ask someone to tell me who and what I am, and then I'll know . . .'

'You are a soft round ball,' said the first person she asked. 'And what you should do is bounce and simply roll along.' So off went the girl, bouncing away and rolling along until she landed – ploof – into the gutter. She managed to crawl out and dragged herself home.

'No, no, no, no, no!' said the next person. 'You are a square box. Firm and hard with sharp corners. You stand square and straight like other boxes.' So, trying to make herself as boxish as she could, she went off to join the other square boxes. But no one seemed to recognise her there and she found herself getting poked and jabbed by the sharp corners of the other square boxes. She tried to smile and stand as firmly and squarely as she could, but she was so dented and bruised that she didn't even appear like a straight, firm square box any more.

The next person told her that she was quite definitely a triangle! There was no doubt about it and she should just balance herself on her tip like a spinning-top. She tried that, and it felt lovely. So she span away round and round and round until she got so dizzy that she lost herself completely. She returned home, feeling sad and lonely. She looked at the blur in the mirror, and no longer knew what to do.

Outside the sun was shining and she decided to go for a walk in the park. 'If I was a tree, I could just grow. If I was a sun, I could simply shine. If I was a bench, I could just wait. But since I don't know what I am, how can I know what I'm supposed to do?' With these thoughts she sat down wearily on the bench and looked around her at people spinning, standing square, bouncing, jumping and flying about. She felt so sorry for herself that she started to cry, and didn't notice that someone else had come to sit on the same bench.

'Isn't it a beautiful day!' said the someone. She stopped crying and turned to find a man sitting beside her. He had a quiet face and smiled a wonderful smile. She smiled back at him, and her own smile warmed her heart and felt so right. The sun shone, the wind blew gently, fluttering the leaves on the tree, and the bench felt still and comforting. Her smile grew.

'You have a beautiful smile!' said the man.

'Thank you,' replied the girl.

The man laughed. 'Why do you thank me?' he said. 'You should thank yourself. Thank the sun, thank the tree, thank life . . .' He continued looking around him.

She suddenly felt very happy and joined his laughter. 'Okay, then, I'll thank them all and thank you, too.'

'All right,' said the man. 'If you thank them all, then you may thank me, too.'

They sat for a while in a comfortable silence, and then the man got up to go. As he was leaving he said to the girl, 'Treasure your smile . . . and be happy,' and he walked away with a light step. The girl stayed on the silent bench, glowing in the warmth of her smile. She looked around her and it seemed as though everything smiled; the sun, the tree, the people, even the wind.

She walked home feeling light. In her room she turned to the mirror and saw the same blur – but also a smile . . .

'What a beautiful smile', she said out loud, and then, as she looked at the smile, a light outline started to emerge around the blur . . .

Leena Dhingra

Leaving Home

Spiked hair wounding the sky with its hard pink tips, she stood against the railings of Tooting Broadway, contemplating the smoke that billowed out of her mouth. With her free hand, she felt absently for a knitted cap in her bag which would swallow up her spikes before she turned the key to the front door. Garish posters advertising 'Dhulan' (Bride), the latest outpouring of cinematic diarrhoea from Bombay, triggered off a nervous twitch in her left eyelid. Weakened by the length and breadth of the strange looks that her skin-tight shiny black trousers were drawing, she inhaled quickly. Butting the cigarette by a smart twist of her booted heel, she walked into Oriental Tandoori and demanded a sweet paan (betel leaf) which she would suck all the way home on the train to absorb the pungent stale smell of smoke on her breath.

She had lived this schizophrenic life ever since she could remember. It was the overlap she was afraid of, the unnoticed leaking of one world into the other. She toyed with her latest idea of leaving home, undaunted by the memory of her past failures. This time it was fool-proof. Mum and Dad weren't so bad really, considering what Shammy was lumbered with – if only their love didn't hover quite so close to oppression, if only they hadn't responded to living here by closing up. Living meekly to put others on the straight and narrow was just not her scene. Anyway, did they really think that Tahir and Sajeda would follow their eldest sister's deviant path? What with their diet of Hindi films and Disco Diwana, that was hardly likely. Huh . . . The red stain of the paan juices gave a fiendish edge to her black painted lips as she relished

32

her latest little plan with a vigorous chomping of paan. This weirdo, she thought with a giggle, was going to ask her parents to approve her marriage to a nice Muslim boy from the same tiny village in Pakistan and, what's more, from a cosy and quite acceptable niche of that hierarchy.

He seemed an okay fella, a bit reticent for a political activist but at least their cultural divide would exclude any possibility of romance. That she could not face. She couldn't even think over the plan in peace in case someone should trespass on her thoughts. Secrecy was so important. As the train rattled into a station where she recognised the ads, she picked up her huge bag and made for the door. She popped into the public loo to do her Cinderella act, whipped out her cleansing cream and cotton wool, wiped off her lipstick, brushed the gel out of her hair and tucked every straying pink wisp into her knitted cap. She pulled out her black T-shirt from her trousers till it hung over her knees, a crumpled but quick churidar kameez. Only the incongruity of black lace-up boots, which had always jarred on her mother's sense of femininity, hinted at what had been.

She walked up the garden path, suddenly noticed the fraying black lace gloves on her hands, tiptoed back a few steps till her silhouette merged with the shadow cast by the overgrown hydrangea and slowly and nimbly removed the gloves so that they would not fray even more. She went for the controlled effect – frayed but not torn. The key had barely turned in the lock when her mother's voice whined out over the Hindi film on the video, 'Zara, is that you?'

'Yes, Mum. Did you think the local cat burglar would use the key?'

'In that skin-tight black churidar, I can hardly be blamed for thinking that. Anyway, what's kept you so late? Your chappatis are in the oven.'

Zara dished out her food. Bhindi, mm, her favourite veg. She'd miss that. It would be eggs and bread after a few days. She took her plate out into the lounge.

'Mind if I eat out here? Promise I won't wipe my hands on the settee.'

'Sh . . . the film's just ending. If the father dies, then the widow can't object to Hema Malini's romance with Dharmendra.'

As the music reached a deafening crescendo, so that the man could breathe his last in time with the music, Zara experimented with opening lines. 'Mum, I'm going to be married. Ammijan, I've found the boy of your dreams. Mummyji.'

The hum of the blank video interrupted her thoughts. 'Where's Dad?'

'At the Islamic Centre. He'll belt you if I tell him what time you came home. You better have a good reason if you want me to keep quiet.'

Zara put her plate down, squeezed in on the armchair between the armrest and her mother, wiped her hands on her mother's dupatta discreetly and said in honeyed tones, 'Mum, I've the best reason in the world and it's so good, I don't mind you telling Dad at all. In fact, you must tell him. A Sunni boy from Ferozepur has proposed to me. His father owns twenty acres of land and Ahmad is the eldest son. And with your permission, I'm going to accept. Now, there's no need to look cross just because I beat you to it and found a more eligible boy than any of your sisters could conjure up.'

Her mother stood up, switched off the TV and, with hands on hips, tried hard not to look pleased. 'So, what's so special about him? You turned down all our suggestions because boys from Pakistan were "Pakis". Anyway, at twenty-one, it's high time you were married. If the boy's from our community and if his background is suitable then I'm sure it will be okay by Dad. What's his family name? Dad can start making enquiries tomorrow.'

'Khan.'

'Oh, Khan. Find out if his father's land is by the railway line. It stretches from the signal box to the first crossing just outside Ferozepur. He might be a cousin. No, don't worry, at least four times removed. That's a good family.' Zara's mum lapsed into counting the generations that had gone between the first blood brothers down to the present day, keeping track of which children belonged to which of the wives.

34

'I'm going to bed,' said Zara with relief. 'It'll take you at least two hours to sort out the family tree. Not quite the kind of gripping stuff which keeps me awake.'

The next morning, after her fortnightly dose of depression at the dole office, she was shocked to find the family assembled in the living-room. Her father's eldest brother and his wife were also present. Her father, looking slightly embarrassed, made the faintest visible gesture of 'come here' with his head and his voice choked on 'beti'. Marriage was not a subject to be easily broached with one's daughter. 'Your uncle knows the family and the boy. The background is okay, but do you know that the boy is seeking political asylum and his application was rejected twice by the Home Office? I hope he isn't going to ditch you after a couple of years. Your uncle and I want to have a chat with him.'

Zara wondered which act to put on. The shock, horror one or the quiet, smug, 'I know all about that' one. The first would've alerted them that this was not quite the madly in love story. So she took the second tack. 'Oh, yes. He's told me the whole story. You know why he's a political refugee though, don't you? His politics are the same as yours Dad, PPP and Benazir Bhutto, Zindabad.'

'He's a PPP man?' Her father smiled approvingly. 'That bastard, Zia, must've made his life intolerable. Right, when are you going to bring your young man home?'

'Whenever you want, Dad.' So the following Sunday was fixed. Ahmad would have lunch there and Zara would have to sit upstairs in her bedroom, after lunch, while the men talked.

That night she phoned Pradeep, Ahmad's friend and middle-man, to arrange a meeting at Pradeep's office the following day. To Pradeep's suspicion-laden voice, Zara whispered, 'Tell you tomorrow,' and hung up.

The next day Zara went up to the City to meet them. Ahmad was there in a kurta pyjama looking irritatingly ethnic, thought Zara, with a maroon embroidered jacket amongst all the City gents. Pradeep took them to a quiet little café round the corner for a beanz on toast meal.

'What's up now?' Pradeep demanded.

'How many apples in a bunch of grapes?' countered Zara.

'Wha . . . at? Be serious.'

'You think I'm silly because I've got no sense?' giggled Zara.

'Look, I don't have much time,' Pradeep's voice rose a threatening decibel or two.

'Well, my dad wants to see Ahmad on Sunday. Lunch at our house and all that. But you can't come. Haven't told the folks about the monkey in the middle – or gooseberry,' she said, looking at his hairy arms.

'Ahmad can't talk about such things. These are delicate matters. He might let the side down. He can talk politics but romance is entirely my forte.'

'You can tell him what to say. But you . . .' Zara said, bringing her two index fingers together in the sign of a cross warding off Dracula, 'you'll bugger it up.'

'Now, listen. If you two are supposed to be staying with me temporarily after marriage, then as best friend I've every right to be there.'

'Okay, okay. But for fucks sake, not a word,' pleaded Zara.

'Language, Lady. There's something else I've got to tell you. You realise that after you marry Ahmad, he won't have any rights here for at least one year. He won't be able to work or claim dole or anything? Now, seeing as he's doing you a favour, helping you to leave home plus we'll both be lying like mad for a year to your family when they call or phone – Zara's in the bath, she's just popped out, she'll call you as soon as she's back . . . Well, that kind of support doesn't come cheap or easy.'

Fear began to creep up Zara's spine into her eyes. 'What do you mean? What are you asking for?'

'£5,000,' said Pradeep triumphantly, noting the fear.

'I don't have that kind of money. You're a friend. You can't do that. People in Ahmad's position pay to arrange a marriage. I'm doing you a favour. You scratch my back and I'll scratch yours.'

'Well, as he'll be staying with me, rent won't be a problem. Okay, £2,500 will do or the whole thing's off.'

'My parents wouldn't let me go to art college and you're not going to stop it either by taking all my savings. Bit pointless leaving home, don't you think?'

'I'm sorry, art college or no, I can't accept less than £1,000. There's plenty of other fish.'

'Suckers . . .' muttered Zara under her breath as her eyes misted up as she thought of her £3,000 in her Abbey National account. So close to success, she couldn't let it slip from her fingers now. She'd just have to live on the grant or make it up in holiday work. What the hell!

'Done,' she said and slapped her hands on Pradeep's outstretched palms.

Sunday dawned. Zara lazed in bed lamenting the precious cheque she had posted to Pradeep. Her thoughts were constantly being punctured by her mother's 'Zara, come and make the salad, Zara, come and do the washing up,' until her sister, Sajeda, her sleep disturbed, answered their mother's call. Finally, with half an hour to go, Zara strolled to the bathroom in her knitted cap to wash the pink dye out of her hair. Out came the silk shalwar, kameez and heavily embroidered dupatta and golden chappals. When she made her appearance downstairs, her mother's delight was apparent as she hugged Zara, saying, 'Even you have your soft spot.' At least it's had the intended effect, Zara thought as she extricated herself from her mother and rearranged her dupatta (scarf).

Lunch was a starchy affair with everyone exchanging meaningful glances with Zara. She thought of the different meanings each person's glance conveyed and suppressed a smile. She swam in and out of the conversation, drowning and, at the same time, feeling that her head was above water, answering, yes or no, as expected of the bride-to-be. In short, exemplary. After lunch, she withdrew to her room as planned and sat on the edge of the bed, biting her nails and hoping that the smell of the incense sticks would hide the smell of cigarette smoke. After two hours, her father called her down. Ahmad and Pradeep had left. Everything was fixed and a buffet lunch would be hosted at the local school hall for three hundred people. Zara sighed with relief.

Tomorrow she would start her own preparations. Whilst her mother grumbled that there was little time to prepare her trousseau, Zara was out visiting her friends to check that the housing association flat had come through, to collect the keys, to look the flat over and to start furnishing it with basics. Over the next few days she bought a secondhand bed and mattress, a gas cooker, a tiny fridge, crockery, etc. Any luxuries like coffee grinders and toasters would hopefully come as wedding gifts. Zara was brimming with excitement. She would open the door to the flat and stand there for five minutes gloating over what was hers, kissing the carpet in a pope-like gesture and fingering the black refuse sacks that were doubling up as curtains. Mine, mine, mine, she thought. Every day a dose of her flat helped to keep her patient and even friendly as her mother dragged her from shop to shop in Southall, worrying about the colour of her gharara, whether imitation pearls or diamonds should be woven in with silk embroidery, the amount of gold in the jewellery and the clothes for Ahmad. Freedom was within grasping distance so Zara held on to her sanity.

As the day drew closer, she phoned Pradeep to make arrangements for transport after the reception. She wanted to leave separately and be driven straight to her flat. Pradeep was furious; protocol had to be maintained. They would have to come together to his house and after that she could change and leave by minicab. She thought that over and sighed. How long this protocol, this etiquette? She screamed silently.

Meanwhile the endless consumerism continued. Her mother was surprised at the ease with which Zara succumbed to her choices for this, 'the' most important day of her life, when she had clung to the knitted cap and lace-up boots for daily dressing beyond the frontiers of good taste and the understanding of lesser mortals like herself. Even a little discussion on shades and matchings, a little argument which lends piquancy to the whole enterprise of shopping, was absent.

It was with the greatest amount of self-restraint that Zara lived through those few days. The impatience that lit her eyes on her wedding day made relatives remark on her radiance. The

38

stream of congratulations, the hugging, the kissing, the smiling made her want to rush to the toilet and do her Cinderella act. Not long now, she thought. When the reception was over, she hugged her family long and hard. This was an unexpected show of emotion from Zara, but then marriage changes a girl, thought her mum indulgently. Ahmad and Zara got into the heavily decorated Mercedes which was being driven by Pradeep. She closed her eyes and laid back in sheer exhaustion.

'Your punk gear is in a carrier bag in the boot,' Pradeep's voice boomed out, forcing her back into the immediate. She felt Ahmad's eyes fix on her and realised that he was still holding her hand.

'Cut it out,' Zara remarked sharply. 'The act's over. Loving bridegroom – that was for public consumption.'

As they drove up to the house, Zara could see a crowd of silhouettes against the net curtains. 'A party,' she gasped. 'Can't face this.'

'Time to celebrate the success of our little plan. You've escaped from home and so has Ahmad.'

'But it's meant to be a secret.'

'It is. Friends think it is a post-reception reception for the younger lot.'

'Exactly what I can't handle now.'

Zara was handed a glass of champagne. 'Sorry, couldn't wait to open the bubbly stuff,' said an eighteen year old looking as if he was about to pass out.

'Be my guest,' Zara's sarcasm was completely wasted.

Pushing her anxieties to an unreachable part of her mind, Zara decided to enjoy herself. At least this crowd wouldn't have any high expectations of propriety from her. By the fourth glass of champagne, Zara was in a bubble; frothing over with relief, tension released, she floated around to the guests she knew in common with Pradeep. Ahmad was tailing her closely, protective groom now that he was no longer prospective. And each time she swayed dangerously forward to make her point forcibly in some random but intent conversation with a guest, she would compensate by going almost as far back on her heels, so that Ahmad's arm shot out and wrapped itself round her midriff. Zara, vaguely aware of pleasure tingling from human touch, pushed at him clumsily, and when she couldn't dislodge him without creating a minor stir, she let his hand stray behind the heavy folds of her pallu. A responsible thought asserted itself. She must stop drinking. This was an unwanted complication. With any other man, she might've said, your bed or mine? For another two hours she hung on to the same drink and desultory strips of conversation, feeling the bubbles sink slowly down to her feet, bringing the heaviness of sobriety in their wake. Eyes bloodshot with fatigue and drink, she made her excuses, which were vulgarly interpreted. With any other man, maybe, she thought as she graciously withdrew, Ahmad in tow.

Pradeep insisted on dropping Zara off. For appearances, Ahmad had to come along. Zara was too tired to complain. When they arrived, Pradeep decided to make coffee for all of them whilst Zara changed in the bedroom. When she emerged, she found Ahmad sitting on the living-room floor with no sign of Pradeep.

'Where's Pradeep?'

'He's gone back to the party.'

'Why did he leave you behind?'

'Because it's our wedding night.' Eyebrows shooting up lustily, he stood up, and before Zara could escape, he had pinned her against the wall. Her knee moved up slowly, deliberately, in a textbook manoeuvre on how to prostrate a male attacker. As he writhed on the floor with the classic symptoms of a man with his balls in a twist, she ran to the bedroom and locked the door. She felt like a heroine in a Hindi movie, only there was no good guy running to her rescue. For an hour or so she heard nothing and wondered whether a knee in the groin could kill. Then she heard him tiptoeing about and with relief, the flat door banging shut.

She didn't particularly feel like venturing out to see whether the door had been closed from the outside. That night, she slept fitfully, nightmares weaving in and out of her sleep, walls parting with riderless horses rearing up near her mattress. She was up at six.

As Zara turned the corner of her short street, two sickeningly familiar figures were lounging against the bus-stand. They ran towards her, each taking her by the arm and squashing her between them, then started walking her away from the tube station down a deserted street. Pradeep panted that he would ring her parents and tell all if she didn't do her wifely bit by Ahmad. A milk van clattered to a halt ten yards from them. Zara stuck her elbows into their sides. As they momentarily loosened their grip, she made a dash for it. The milkman's suspicious glances rooted them to the spot, looking sheepish and unsure.

Zara took the tube into central London. She needed to be surrounded by people. Amongst that throbbing mass of people rushing to work, Zara's aimless wandering made her feel as if she would be trampled underfoot at any time. She had been born into the wrong time and space. She stepped sideways into a newsagent's and hung around the magazine rack behind the glass frontage through which the sea of people heaved sickeningly into a tidal wave. Her eyes caught the word *Asha* (hope). She picked up the magazine, a monthly for Asian women. She'd never seen a magazine for Asians before, at least not one published here, only those imports from the sub-continent which her mother bought. There was a whole new world waiting here, some of it impinging directly on her life. Going through the classified section, she noticed an ad, for a community centre – advice and counselling offered to Asians on immigration, welfare rights, marital problems, the works. Well, what about this, then? she mused. She had reached a dead end. She had messed up even this carefully planned escape. She had to seek help. She hoped that the centre was not run by Pakistanis, in case someone recognised her. She paid for the magazine and walked back to the station.

By coincidence, the woman at the centre was also called Asha. Zara's path seemed to be littered with hope-laden omens. Asha's friendly eyes hardened after a surreptitious glance at Zara's hair. Zara looked at the rings on her well-manicured fingers and thought bitterly, appearances do after all bear some relation to reality. Asha listened to Zara in fascination, as if hooked by the decadence of this generation of Asian girls. 'I think you have made a serious mistake. There are two ways out of this. You have misunderstood the depth of parents' love in our culture. They were only trying to do their best for you by giving you a comfortable, secure home and planning a good marriage for you. By going your way, you've landed yourself in hot water. Go back and ask their forgiveness. If you like, I can talk to them. The other way is to go back to your husband. After all, he was only demanding his rights, nothing unreasonable. When you take your vows, they've got a right to expect something in return.'

Zara walked away, head bowed, dragging her feet, all exits closed.

'You win some, you lose some,' Asha sighed. 'Poor girl. Don't know what's going wrong nowadays. Our girls want too much like these *gorais* (whites) they go to school with.'

Zara couldn't go back to her flat. It wasn't safe. She couldn't go home. Her head swam with the events of the last two days. She needed to sleep. Somewhere, from the corner of her eye, she could see soft, green grass nodding away into the horizon. Would she dare? A street tramp. What would her family say? She walked, undecided, towards that inviting patch. A contemptuous sneer from a well-dressed passer-by decided it for her. What the hell! I am the pits, in any case, she thought, as she closed her eyes.

When she woke up, the day was not quite finished. The sun was shining miles away from the horizon. It was only seven. What would she do between now and nightfall? When was the best time to return to her flat? She was hungry. She went back to the footpath and walked towards the shops. Stopping at a Wimpy, she picked up a hamburger and, as the first bite sank into the depths of her stomach, she decided that a well-paced pint of beer could easily take her up to ten o'clock. With that pleasant thought filling her up warmly, she started looking around for a familiar sign.

'Hey you! Oi you,' someone shouted from across the road. Zara only half registered this as she was still engrossed in her search for a pint. That someone was sprinting across. 'Hey, Zara, didn't I go to school with you?' Zara looked at her, 'Suri, am I glad to see you,' and hugged her warmly, as if they were long-lost friends. Suri

42

stood, embarrassed, not sure if their acquaintance merited such a warm reception.

'Look, I need your help desperately. I'll tell you about it over a drink.'

At the Cock and Bull, Zara launched into her narrative about Ahmad's furtive passion for her. Suri was overcome. When she had finished, Suri hugged her till the tears came streaming down Zara's face in remembrance of things past. 'Look, I'm working for this women's centre that some of us black women helped set up. We'll get you out of this mess.'

Zara looked wary. 'I know all about you lot. Go home, you'll say. Do you know Asha? Sorry, mate, can't take up your offer.'

'Meet me tomorrow at 11.00 sharp. Not taking no for . . .'

'Suri, where will I hang out between now and tomorrow? Can't go home,' Zara hissed between clenched teeth.

'Oh, God, yes! You could come and kip in my lounge, I s'pose, till you sort yourself out.' Zara's relief was so total that the slight note of reluctance in Suri's offer went unnoticed.

Next morning, Zara trudged grudgingly up to the centre with Suri, her pessimism not uplifted by the peeling unmarked door, squashed between a takeaway and a newsagent. Suvarna, Suri's co-worker, was waiting for them at the top of the dingy stairs.

Sitting around an electric heater, Suvarna listed the options briskly. 'Right, your first need is housing. Can't go back there. I'm going to ring up the council, get you on to their homeless list. You should be able to get bed and breakfast tonight, but getting a flat may take up to six months. Being a black woman helps. Being single with no kids, doesn't. When they ask about violence, say he kicked you around. They don't recognise rape in marriage, so don't talk about his roving hands. If you don't fancy the council option, get on to your housing association, explain the situation and ask if they'll exchange the flat for somewhere else.'

'Third,' Suri butted in, 'come and kip out in my lounge whilst you're sorting yourself out.'

'Now, the next thing you need to do is to take out an injunction so he can't touch you. It's not quite as easy as it sounds. It can take ages and if he's untameable he might still try, and it's very hard to get the police to enforce it. Considering his immigration problems, he might lie low with an injunction waving around in his face. There is another way of putting him out of reach. Far, far more effective. But it's an option I can't help you with. It would be politically against my principles. But women in DV cases . . .'

'Sorry?' interrupted Zara.

'In domestic violence cases, women have written to the Home Office revealing how theirs was a marriage of convenience and got their husbands deported. But, as we also get involved in campaigns against the immigration laws, I can't help you there. However, threatening to use that last resort might get your money back. And you'll need that little nest-egg while you're looking for work.'

'Thanks Su. It's been wonderful talking to you. Just one last thing. My parents. If Pradeep squeals, I'll have lost them for ever.'

'That is entirely up to them. I can ring them if you like, and tell them your side of the story. But whether that opens or shuts doors is another matter altogether.'

'Okay. I'll handle that side of it. Can I use your phone?'

Zara dialled Pradeep's office number with a joy she hadn't felt for some time, the joy of having the upper hand.

'Thought you'd come round eventually, sweetheart. A bit quick on the uptake, though,' crooned Pradeep smugly.

'That't right. I'd like my money back in full, no expenses deducted. You wouldn't want to drive your dear friend to Heathrow to catch the next flight back to Pakistan, now, would you?' said Zara thickly in a one-up-to-me voice. She caught Pradeep saying, 'Your parents already know . . .' as she put the receiver gently back into its cradle.

'That was the sweetest connection British Telecom ever allowed me to make. Thanks,' said Zara squeezing Su and Suri's hands.

That evening, accompanied by Suri, Zara dared to visit her flat, pick up her belongings and shift to Suri's. As she opened the door, she saw an envelope addressed to her in a handwriting that made her heart jump. 'Mum,' she whispered and tore open the envelope.

Darling Zara,
Pradeep rang us today and gave us your address. We know everything. If we had only realised that you wanted to leave home that badly . . . As long as the relatives think you are still married, we won't lose face. Please contact us.

Carrying a suitcase and three carrier bags, they made their way to the nearest unvandalised call box and joined the queue.

Rahila Gupta

The Debt

The plane was preparing to land. The captain's voice was muffled, but clear enough to ignite a rush of activity up and down the plane as everyone set about locating bits of hand luggage, retrieving seatbelts from under sleeping travelling companions, searching out lost shoes, or making a quick run for the loo. Freshen up pads doubled as waken up pads and finally all the plane's babies started to cry simultaneously, obliterating the last pieces of the captain's information and making sure that those who hadn't quite awakened now did so.

The young woman at the windowseat on row P appeared to be the only one not participating in the bustle around her. Instead, she sat packed and prepared, still and silent, gazing out of the small window. So still in fact that one could have imagined her to be asleep if it weren't for her alert posture and intent gaze as she peered out at the plane staircasing down through the clouds. When the plane leap-plunged she held her chest and smiled – and stayed in that posture until it finally landed and stopped, whereupon she pulled out a camera from the bag in her lap and snapped a series of quick shots. Then, leaning back in her chair, she let out a loud, long sigh.

Anjali Datta, twenty years old, was arriving in India as she had done many times before, but this was a special arrival – for the first time she was arriving on her own. Arriving as a grown-up, as an independent, autonomous, professional – well, nearly professional – at any rate, a person in her own right. It was all really a bit of a dream come true, and everything, but everything matched and mirrored her feelings – the plane's leaps were like the leaps of her own heart, the pressure in the ears only served to heighten the already intense drone in her head which blocked out the world, and finally the dreamlike quality of the heat rising and quivering tenuously in the piercing sunlight encapsulated it all – she reached for her camera and quickly snapped it.

When the doors opened and the heat poured in she felt quite overwhelmed and imagined herself to be rising, floating, enveloped in warmth . . .

'When we arrived, I felt light-headed and dazed in a haze of heat,' She made a mental note to remember the formulation 'haze of heat' as she squeezed into the line filing its way out of the plane, much too slowly . . . 'I really can't describe the feelings of the arrival. I was quite calm until we landed, and then I could hardly contain my excitement and restlessness to rush – out out out – and into the sun . . . of INDIA!'

Anjali had long developed this way of voicing in her head simultaneous running commentaries of events and feelings. They took different forms and served different functions – they could be in the form of letters, a part of a story, in the first or third person, and ever since she had gone to film school, they had developed into all different kinds of voice-over styles. They served as a sort of emotional safety valve, a way of distancing, sharing, releasing intensities of emotion.

Once outside, the haze of heat was in actuality a glare blast. She groped her way down, squinting and hanging on to the handrail. But when her feet touched the ground, 'Oooohh!' she let out an involuntary squeal of delight, and automatically coughed to cover it up. 'Ah, but no!' she thought, 'I don't need to cover things any more. This is India, where I don't need to hide, for it's where I belong!' She bent down to scrape up a pinch of dust, and would have liked to lift it to her forehead in a gesture of reverence – but felt too shy. Instead she gripped it between her fingers and quickly flowed back into the stream of travellers. Of course, the old freedom fighters wouldn't have felt shy, she thought, and she tried to wonder what they would have felt – elation? joy? sacrifice? duty? destiny? – and which of these found an echo within her.

47

Anjali felt close to the freedom fighters and sometimes even imagined herself to be one. For though of course now India was free from the colonialist yoke, she had been taught that this was only the beginning and that much needed to be done before the fruits of that freedom could be reaped by all, for then and only then would India be healed and restored to her former glory! Brought up most of her life in the West, she had been fed on the diet of expatriates: of dreams and longing, of stories and legends and the whole larger-than-life dimension created by distance and desire. Her parents' feelings had transposed and she had grown up with the idea that she had a kind of duty . . . a mission . . . almost a debt . . . to India. This return held so much promise. She tripped along happily, adding a purposefulness to her gait and watching her reflection in the smoked glass of the airport building.

'Miss Anjali Datta from the UK?'

Anjali nodded energetically.

'I am V P Sharma. I have come from Dr Malhotra to bring you there. *Namaste.*'

'Oh, thank you. *Namaste*,' replied Anjali and as she hastily brought her palms together in the appropriate gesture the dust from her clenched fingers fell . . .

Mr Sharma took over, managing the luggage, and Anjali happily followed without even stopping to wonder how it was she had been located in the crowded terminal building. As far as she was concerned it was just part of the magic of India! Yes, like the wonderful web of family, family friends, and friends of family friends. The magic that had enabled her to come, unchaperoned, to an unknown city – for Bombay was virtually unknown – with a purpose of her very own, and an actual job to go to – she squealed involuntarily.

'*Han ji.* Yes? Did you say something?'

'No, no, I'm just happy to be here.'

'*Accha.* That is good,' smiled Mr V P Sharma.

The car drove along, and Anjali looked around her at the 'here' which appeared to be sea, sky, skyscrapers and slums.

'When you grow up you will go back to work in India.' She remembered her mother's voice. 'There is so much that needs to be done . . . so many people that need to be helped . . .' She was moved – by the memory and the realisation that she was here, at last, all ready and raring to go – to fulfil her own 'tryst with destiny!'

Anjali pulled out her camera and kept it ready in her lap, just in case, for any memo snaps. She then placed her imaginary camera in the front seat, angled, so that it framed her side profile looking out of the window. It was a documentary with her own voice-over:

'I decided to study film and media, basically because of the tremendous power of the visual image to communicate, educate, enlighten – to change. I always intended to come back and work in India, to make my contribution, to do something that would be of relevance . . . benefit . . . to the Indian masses. If my science grades had been any good I would have chosen medicine, or agriculture . . .'

'Cut,' she decided, as she smiled at the lie, recalling her squeamishness of blood and needles.

'But now, at last, I am here!' And she settled back into her seat to feel the sea breeze and to savour once again the set of circumstances that had combined and conspired to make this arrival possible. Pure magic!

It had all happened because Uncle Raj, an old family friend who had come to stay for a few days, had fallen ill, and so had had to stay a few weeks instead. Being housebound, he had to be visited, and so there came on the scene his network of family friends and friends of family friends, amongst whom there was someone who, in turn, had a family friend of his own who knew a man in Bombay making educational films for rural development. Combined with that, Anjali, now in her final year at film school, was looking for a professional placement for work experience. So letters were exchanged, calls made, it was learned that a new project was starting in which Anjali could participate, the director of the film school thought it was an excellent idea, and they were all smiles as everything was finalised. Uncle Raj stopped over in Bombay on his return to tie up the details of Anjali's stay, which was to be with old Dr Malhotra, a doctor from old Lahore who was a family friend to them all.

'It really was a most amazing example of the right people, the right place and the right time,' Anjali had squealed delightedly down the telephone to a friend.

'Good luck and Karma,' corrected her mother. 'Whatever happens is God's will, and never forget to say thank you.'

Anjali smiled as she remembered, and opened her eyes to blink a thank you to the sky.

'Aha. You have awakened,' said V P Sharma. 'That is good, because we are nearly now arriving.'

Anjali pulled herself up to look. The scene had changed. The car inched its way along the congested street straight into and through the lives of people whose homes – hardly homes, refuges more likely – were along the pavements. Whole families huddled around bundles containing their meagre possessions, covered in dust and treated like dust, attempting to get on with the business of survival between the feet of the pedestrians, the fumes of the vehicles and competing for space and scraps with the stray dogs and cats.

Anjali let out a cry of dismay.

'Yes, they come from the countryside to Bombay,' explained Mr Sharma.

'From where? And why?'

'Yes, and they keep coming,' returned Mr Sharma.

The car stopped at the traffic light. Next to a flashy food hall disgorging satisfied customers sat a bewildered group of mother and three children. The juxtaposition of images was such that Anjali automatically reached for her camera, but as she started to lift it her eyes caught a look . . . a stare? . . . a glare? It pierced through her – she froze, her camera held halfway to her chest. As the car jolted forward, she relaxed it back into her lap and she tried to decipher the look . . . its meaning . . . her feelings . . .

At Dr Malhotra's, Anjali was met by Elizabeth, who took

over from V P Sharma. A brisk, bright-eyed old woman, she immediately poured forth a stream of information as she led Anjali through the apartment towards the sitting-room. The Doctor sahib, it turned out, had been called out of station with return delayed till tomorrow. But Anjali's room was ready, her bath water hot, and she could have a bath first and then tea, or tea first and then bath. Uncle Raj had called a few times and would be doing so again later, as indeed would Dr Malhotra, and the party she had come to visit would be sending a car for her the next day at four. She then went on to explain to Anjali, her tone conspiratorial, that she had been called down especially to be with Anjali, that normally she lived in Poona with Dr Malhotra's daughter, whom she had looked after for the last thirty years, ever since the child was two, and was regarded as one of the family.

'. . . So when you are coming the Doctor sahib come to me. "Elizabeth," he say, "I have a young girl from England and only manservant without English." I tell him no problem, I come.' She looked at Anjali knowingly. 'You come for meeting with party here? Yes?' and stopped talking for the first time.

'Yes,' replied Anjali. 'And I do speak Hindi,' she added firmly to set the record straight – she recalled the sweat and tears with which she had scraped her Hindi 'O' level, reminding herself of the freedom fighters, their courage and . . . her debt.

'That is very good,' replied Elizabeth, bustling off to attend to something.

Anjali strolled out on to the terrace, trying to get a sense of . . . everything. The image of the little street boy appeared before her, and the look in his eyes, which she was beginning to regard as a sign . . . trying to say something to her . . . it was the stare, so expressionless, yet so eloquent. Like her mother said, there really was so much to be done in India. Her eyes misted over; she wiped them on the sleeve of her shirt as Elizabeth returned.

'Oh, ho, Anjaliji, Babyji, what is there to cry about? You should not cry.' Elizabeth spoke in Hindi, gently, with empathy, and brushing aside Anjali's attempt to explain, she

51

continued, with a touch of indignation in her tone, 'I will come with you to meet the party tomorrow, or better still call the party here when the Doctor sahib gets back.' To Anjali's bewildered look she replied, 'Come, come now. You go and have a bath while I bring you tea. Don't worry about anything.'

The combination of the hot bath, sea air, jet lag and tea made Anjali dozy. She floated away into a timeless space of simultaneous dreaming, waking, sleeping, not knowing which was which, but during which she imagined herself to be making quantum leaps of awareness and understanding – with the look in the eyes guiding, teaching, transforming and sometimes merging with those of Elizabeth, who always appeared at hand . . . solicitous, tending, concerned.

Anjali awoke from her fourteen hours sleep feeling fresh and alert though still locked in the night's feeling of timelessness.

'A rather wonderful feeling of great stillness.' She started her imaginary letter. 'As I drank my tea on the veranda on my first full day in India, I understood for the first time why time is deified. Why it is called "Great Time". There definitely is something . . .'

Elizabeth interrupted her with her own commentary about who'd called when, and why she'd ordered English lunch . . .

The mention of lunch brought Anjali back to clock time: she had three and a half hours before her meeting with Mr Mathur of Apex Films. Just about enough time to get ready at leisure. She relaxed back into her thoughts.

'Mahā Kāla,' she murmured softly to herself, pleased that she had retrieved the word from her memory store.

'What did you say?' Elizabeth looked puzzled.

'I said, Mahā Kāla, Great Time. You know, it's one of the names of the Great God Shiva, and I had been trying to remember it.'

Looking increasingly puzzled, Elizabeth replied by offering once again to accompany Anjali to the afternoon's meeting – an idea which Anjali firmly dismissed with some irritation.

The car arrived on time. The driver came up and rang the

doorbell. Anjali was ready to leave. Elizabeth looked anxious as she watched her go.

'I'll be back soon!' said Anjali cheerily. 'You'll see. Before anyone calls again or Doctor sahib arrives.'

Elizabeth nodded, unconvinced.

Zipping along in the car, Anjali again thought about Time, about the Great Goddess Kāli, who was all powerful because she was the Goddess of Time, about the little street boy with his large, silent, staring eyes, about her destination, about what sort of a man Mr Mathur would be and what she should call him: Mr Mathur? Uncle? Mathurji? She decided the last one best suited someone engaged in rural development. 'Rural development,' she asked the sky, 'means the development of the countryside, doesn't it?' She conjured up the image of the boy with the silent eyes, and felt so moved that she spoke out loud. 'If the countryside were developed you wouldn't have to come here like a beggar to grovel in the filth.' The driver threw a backward glance, but Anjali was lost in her thoughts. Rural development! Clean drinking water! Land to till! Irrigation canals! The eyes assumed a look of gratitude. Her sense of purpose grew. She felt aglow with goodwill! She felt – a chosen one! Yes, like Joan of Arc must have felt when she heard the voices!

'Driving along in the car to my destination, I felt almost as though I was driving towards my own destiny. Ready to meet it, ready to learn, ready to grow . . .'

The car stopped. The engine was turned off.

'Gosh!' she exclaimed, 'Are we already there?'

The lift took her to the top floor and opened straight into the plush offices of Apex Films. Anjali let out a little gasp of surprise but before there was time to recover, she was thrown into another.

'Anjali!' A dashing-looking man around thirty strode towards her. 'So good to meet you at last.'

This wasn't quite what Anjali had expected. 'Are you . . . Mr Mathur . . . I mean Mathurji?' She stammered slightly.

He laughed. 'That's right, but there's no need for that formality. Just call me Matty, everyone else does.'

As he waltzed Anjali through to the inner office, he explained the history of his name. How when he was studying in America it

53

used to get pronounced to sound like Matthew . . . how he'd stopped correcting it . . . got used to it and it had just stuck and then even got shortened to Matty. Anjali noted the American twang in his voice but quickly arrested the thought, blaming it on her prejudiced English education. She herself was determined to be open minded and open hearted.

'Will you have tea, lemon juice or coconut water?' he offered. His smile was disarming.

Anjali slunk into the sofa to wait for the coconut water, delighting in the attention, her host's engaging ways, the comfortable elegance of her surroundings, and the wonderful sea view. She closed her eyes and threw another thank you to the sky.

'So, you want to come back and work in India?' Matty sat down in the swivel chair.

Anjali nodded.

'Good, good. There's a lot that needs to be done and a lot of scope. I liked your work . . . very promising.'

He really was so eminently huggable, thought Anjali as she tried to contain her childish squeals.

'Gosh, thank you,' she managed.

'Well, here, at Apex, we do a mixture of work. We do some advertising films, and we also take on contracts from the government. So the work is therefore both varied and interesting. In India you see, film really works. The people are very open . . . almost gullible . . . and it is a very powerful and persuasive medium.'

Anjali nodded. 'I am particularly interested in rural development,' she threw in.

'Quite right, quite right. That is a most important factor and one you will be working on. The team you will be with are away in the field and will be back in two days when you will meet them and be plunged straight into work.'

'Oh, good.'

'You see, in India we have everything. We have the technology, we have the know-how, we have the personnel and we have the manpower. We are the eighth biggest industrial nation and we need to project ourselves into the next century and take our rightful place in the world. What has been holding us back is centuries of tradition and ignorance – and these need to be rooted out.'

'Tradition?'

'What's that?'

'I said, tradition?'

'Yes, that's right, and ignorance.' He swivelled his chair. 'Now, we have been given a large contract by the government. They are planning to build a large reactor in the interior around which, eventually, an industrial complex will grow. We have been commissioned to make a series of educative films to help pave the way. These will then be disseminated by satellite to the countryside around.' He offered Anjali a cigarette. 'No? You don't mind if I do?' Anjali shook her head. 'You see, these lands have traditionally been held by certain tribal groups and small farmers and these people will now have to move.'

'Does that mean they will be dispossessed?' interrupted Anjali.

'They will be – resettled.'

'Where?'

'The whole project will develop over a considerable period of time and many things will change by then. The point of the film is to help that change and to help the people adjust to the change. You get me?'

Anjali nodded unsurely.

'What you must understand is that this is progress – and that is what must be communicated through the films. They must be persuasive and reassuring.' He assumed a reassuring tone. 'It will provide work for the area because the labour of the local people will be required to build it and in this way they will be involved in participating in the change.'

'And when it's all built, what will happen to the people then?'

'Ah, that will be a long time yet. Many will be absorbed in the new complex and the others will be . . . resettled.'

'I see,' murmured Anjali.

'Progress has a price. Sometimes a heavy price, a very heavy price, indeed!' He smiled his disarming smile. Anjali now saw it as smarmy. A price which you will never have to pay, she thought as she surveyed the room.

'We cannot afford to be sentimental,' he cautioned. 'I think you will enjoy the challenge, because one of the things we have to do is to teach, to impart some of the most basic concepts of progress, concepts which you and I take for granted, but which to these simple, rural people are quite new and will transform their whole reality.' He reached out for a file. 'Like this – you'll probably be working on this one so you can take it to look through – it's about time.'

'Time?'

'Yes, about teaching the concept of time. The idea that time is money!'

Anjali jolted.

'Surprised, huh? Well, you see how a simple idea like that, which we take for granted, has to be clearly put over. That time is money is one of the basic concepts necessary for progress, and you have to . . .'

Anjali's head reeled. Time is money! Confusion . . . incomprehension. She heard no more.

Driving in the car, she had no memory of when she'd got in. The file in her lap, she lifted and placed on the seat beside her. She looked absently through the sky and saw the eyes looking at her, trying to say something – she didn't want to hear and dispelled the image by consciously taking note of the passing people, shops, cars, buildings, hoardings . . . until she finally arrived at Dr Malhotra's.

Elizabeth was at the door; her face became grave as she saw Anjali.

'Go sit,' she ordered. 'I'll bring tea.'

Anjali sat, feeling heavy and dulled. Even the commentaries in her head were silent. She could make no sense of her feelings. The image of the eyes reappeared, the look asserted itself and said, 'Traitor!'

'No, no, no!' she called out. 'No! No! And go away!'

Elizabeth rushed into the room exclaiming, 'Anjaliji! Baby! Are you all right?'

Anjali composed herself. 'I'm all right. It's just . . .'

'You're not all right.' Elizabeth was indignant. 'You should never have gone on your own. I told you not to! It's not proper anyway! I heard you say no, and you must say no! You must not marry a man you don't like.'

Anjali was transfixed. Her chin quivered as she was just about to burst – into laughter, she thought – until Elizabeth gently gathered her into her arms, and she found herself dissolving into uncontrollable sobs.

Leena Dhingra

A Beginning and an End

Living in England, news from home gets distorted by distance and time and expectations. What started as a pimple on my mother's face gradually became a cancerous sore – not in time or by medical default but by the staggered way in which the news was filtered through to me. An aunt invited me to dinner to give me the news. They didn't want to write to you, she said, in case you faint from shock – a logic which immediately raised my suspicions. I don't understand why I should be shocked by a pimple on which they will operate. The word 'operation', however, had its sobering effect – but why a pimple, why this interest in plastic surgery at this time of life? I was asked to visit, to return 7,000 miles, to borrow money for my fare – and I thought, no, it's a pimple, I'll stay till after the summer sales and pay my fare with my overtime earnings.

Not being able to penetrate my unfrightened state without frightening me, relatives could not persuade me to go. So they resurrected the truth in one short cruel statement. Took the next flight out. A request for liquid food. She wrote and asked for powdered, easy-to-make soups. I took 175 packets in my enthusiasm to please – at one a day, they outlived her by four. Bulk quantities of every minor request as if she would be obliged to live until she finished each item. My mother hated waste.

I risked the wrath of the Bombay customs. Each Knorr packet tucked between books and knickers. Customs saw the books, saw the passport. Thought, student! Thought, British! Chewed paan but wouldn't put the clearance chalk marks on my suitcase. I looked through the smoked-up glass twenty yards away and saw a hand above the sea of heads – long, tapering fingers reduced to

58

bones, consumed by the lengthening shadow of disease but still the hand that had stung my adolescent cheek. My eyes poked into that rattling skeletal hand, searching for clues of what the face might have become, afraid to confront the evidence directly. Will she have time to recognise what I have become? Looked at the customs man, saw perversity and thought, Bastard! My mother is dying. And all the time the restless skeleton caught my eye.

At home, a shabby depressed home. I meet my closest best friend and cannot proceed beyond 'Hello!' I look at her and weep and weep . . .

I had come home, she had to go abroad. A crippling trip abroad. Hospital after specialist hospital. No, we can't treat you. Go home. Just like that. Not even a word of comfort to raise hopes crushed and money humiliatingly borrowed, so ill-spent. And all because an Indian doctor said, unguardedly, in America there is this new drug, platinum.

She was returning. Found a hospital which would cater for her dying needs. That day, I woke up early. The alarm was set for seven, but at a quarter to six I was fumbling for the lightswitch, dispelling dreams of a clear-skinned face, the scars gone, the pus-filled wounds dry – only the shadow of what was fell across her face. Half-asleep, stumbled to the phone to check on arrival time. Walked to the corner to buy a cigarette. Ambulance arrived on time, trusted man ready to leave me behind. I fight with him, you could've picked me up at the corner. The ambulance is not a taxi, he mutters.

Two hours late, the plane taxis down to the waiting ambulance. Red carpet laid out to the plane, a bit musty and torn but red all the same. Stretcher carried up. My friend asks if she can follow, she has never seen the inside of a plane before. Ghostly emptiness of rows of seats and littered aisles except by an emergency exit where an intent group of people huddle. I cannot see her, I break down. I know that early morning dreams are never true. The air hostess keeps me supplied with tissues and whispered condolences. Unthinking, tear-blinded, I stoop to kiss her bandaged face, flashing by so quickly, arresting my need for physical contact in mid-air, adding to embarrassment when the bearer admonishes, 'Later,' as if spontaneity can be put off.

Trip back to the hospital in a jolting ambulance – a painful anticipation of potholes. Trying to keep her from sliding off the stretcher, dividing attention unequally so as not to notice her decline. Catching her breath, she says, 'I nearly died last night.' If not for an emergency injection, my father tells me later. It is that 'nearly' that is peculiar to her condition, an inch closer always but never at the end.

Hospital: endless corridors, trolley careering madly down in chase of the elusive doctor on duty. Admit her, admit her, please. An endless wait, hunger and inefficiency. Peon waiting mealy-mouthed for baksheesh.

Finally, a cold white room, peeling the sticky nylon sari from her bones and removing shoes hanging limply on her feet. Finally, the most pressing problem over. Pessaries, long-awaited catharsis, purgation ripping her bowels clean. What a long night punctuated by cigarette burns and forty winks. Consoling myself with truisms, time flies. After every hour, a minute passes. She is not even troublesome enough to help me pass the time. Reading *Sound and Fury*, letting words flow over me, meaningless music jarring my tired senses. Minutes collecting on my lids, shortening the gaps between my ever-drooping lashes. Give her sleep, she needs it. I must fight it.

Rahila Gupta

A Letter Long Overdue

I We have not yet met
but your face is familiar

Gathering sticks
or growing mielies
on the bare hillsides
of arid Bantustans –
'homelands' that are not home.

In the townships
folding, unfolding
your plastic shacks
at dawn, at dusk.

While in the cities
you clean their homes
cook their meals
tend their children

Your own lives
signed and sealed
stamped and dated.

II We remember
our yesterdays:
they cannot be forgotten.
They broke the thumbs
of our weavers,
they forced our peasants
 to plant indigo
that made the land barren –
only their greed grew.

Now we meet them
on their ground here –
in the famous square
with its fountains and galleries
we stand at the foot
of this monstrous white edifice,
we shout and chant
and our police, like yours
make arrests, and move us on.

III In the supermarkets,
grapes, oranges, pineapples,
sun-ripened, opulent flesh
from your sweat and blood
spilt on the stolen soil of Cape
and the Orange Free State.

In Soweto, Crossroads, Mamelodi,
bulldozers crush your homes,
tear-gas sweeps the dust,
the 'hippos' cruise the streets.
With stinging eyes
your children,
Azania,
rise against the guns
and fight back.

Sibani Raychaudhuri

The Great Escape

        I was new to Great Britain. New to the culture of the mother and toddler groups. Initially it was strange, huddling together at coffee mornings with other women whose entrance ticket was the toddler clinging to the skirt. But I soon realised the importance of these groups. They were venues where British mothers supported, comforted, sympathised, exaggerated and exulted with each other. The bizarrest of tales were narrated, believed and enjoyed: defiant adventures in the thick of mothering. This was possibly the only place where mothers could let their hair and their toddlers down while battling through toddlerdom.

I was therefore not surprised when Anne suddenly burst into the weekly mother and toddler group with a tale that could not wait. 'Look,' she commanded, pulling up a chair to join the circle and thrusting her ten pale, podgy fingers in front of our faces. 'I've found them at last.'

Exchanging discreetly puzzled glances with the others, I thought about the great strides that modern medicine and plastic surgery were making in the West.

'Found them on top of the old cupboard,' Anne continued with deep satisfaction. 'Been looking for them for a week. Must have put them there to keep them out of Tom's reach.' She nodded to emphasise. 'In desperation I rang Mum. Mum said nothing but a prayer to St Andrew, the family saint, would do and that she would go off in the afternoon, say a prayer and give an offering. Do you know that I found them that very evening, just as Mum had finished praying to St Jude.' She flashed her large blue eyes intently on the group, pushing in the proof of St Jude's powers.

I noticed that everyone was trying to look at Anne's hands but she had, in the gusto of recounting, curled them up and stuck them under her thighs.

'Let's see them again,' said Fay, the boldest in the group.

'There,' said Anne, spreadeagling her fingers. 'My wedding ring, my engagement ring, my former engagement ring and this little silver ring which I've worn since I was sixteen.'

Disappointment and relief mingled. Disappointment that Anne had misplaced only her rings and not her fingers. But relief, too, that I would not have to figure out how human fingers could stay fresh for a week on top of a cupboard.

Shortly after the riddle of rings and fingers was solved my new friend Caroline and I wheeled our toddlers, Richard and Priya, out of the playgroup to Caroline's flat. We had met at the playgroup over several weeks and now she had invited me home for lunch. Arriving at her mansion block, Caroline opened the door to her flat and pushed Richard in his buggy down her hall while I gathered Priya and her paraphernalia. As I shuffled towards Caroline's apartment she came out saying, 'Let me give you a hand.' Almost on cue a mischievous kick of air slammed the door shut.

'Oh, no!' exclaimed Caroline. 'The keys are inside.'

Mesmerised by the fear that Richard would fall down the flight of stairs at the end of the hall, we coaxed, cajoled, shouted and begged Richard through the letter slit to 'be a clever boy and hand Mummy the keys from the table', but to no avail. He soon lost interest in our fingers dancing through the slit and our desperate imitations of animals, birds and moving objects. Thinking of a duplicate set of keys, Caroline, flushed with new hope, went down to the caretaker, who lived in the basement. As luck would have it, she was out.

Caroline then tried to ring her husband to come home and open the flat. But being lunchtime William wasn't in either. The only way out was for Caroline to ring Emergency. As she panted up the stairs I was relieved to hear that help was on its way, though I did think that I heard the jingling of a rattle intermittently. In minutes a fire engine with a team of bustling men were there, questioning us as to how it happened, the doors to the flat, whether gas or electricity was on, were the taps turned off, etc, etc. After hearing Richard was eighteen months old they decided to break open the door right away.

'The door doesn't allow a second's delay where children are concerned. Show me the fire exit to your flat. Don't want to break down the main door, do we?' said one of them, oddly jubilant. Caroline dutifully led us all to the back of the building and up several flights of stairs to the fire exit doors. The maze of stairs and doors looked like the setting of *West Side Story* while the residue of daily living tied up in plastic bags to be thrown away cluttered the place.

'That's the door,' pointed Caroline.

'All right, boys,' said the fireman in charge. 'Break it down.' Several of them lunged at the door with a round heavy wooden shaft. With a protracted scream the door gave way, revealing a tiny man sitting on the pot, his mouth open in frozen protest and embarrassment. Oblivious of his presence the firemen rushed in, looking for Richard. Caroline, now able to get a good view of the man performing ablutions, wailed, 'Oh, it's the wrong flat! Ours is the one on top. We live above the Japanese family.'

The firemen took this piece of information in their stride and blowing a 'sorry about this, governor,' trampled off. Clump, clump, their boots meeting the iron stairs, while the wooden shaft, silently, magically, was snaked up to the floor above. A moment's hesitation as one of the firemen asked Caroline 'Are you sure you live here, lady?' Then the loud crunch of another door vanquished. This time it was the right door and in seconds a sleepy Richard was brought to Caroline in a fireman's arms. He had managed the stairs all right and had fallen asleep while playing.

Caroline, relieved and bursting with gratitude, shouted, 'Everyone for tea?' when the entrance of a burly, navy-blue clad policeman caught everyone's attention.

'You'd better go down,' he said gently to Caroline, 'and look after your husband. He's just arrived from the office and fainted when he heard he'd have to pay for both the fire exit doors. Make HIM a cup of tea, love.'

William was supported in a few minutes later, heralded by

the caretaker, who had also arrived by then. The shrill calls of the whistling kettle announced that water was boiling.

As we all sat around the kitchen table for tea it was the policeman who broke the reverie of satisfaction that no real damage had been done. Little Richard, after all, was safe and sound. 'But the wrong door was broken down, I'll need some details,' he said. Turning to Mrs Bond, the caretaker, he asked with one raised eyebrow, 'The name of the gentleman in question?'

'Mr Higashi-i-riki,' said Mrs Bond in a superior manner, proud at the opportunity to show off her mastery of foreign names.

'Spelt in the usual way, I presume,' said the policeman, pencilling in something into his notebook.

After tea I prepared to leave. 'See you next week,' said Caroline, waving goodbye. 'Good story for the M and T group,' she said.

'That's right,' I replied. Mind over Trouble.

This is an extract from a novel called *London Journal* which I am writing.

Kanta Talukdar

Baby Talk I

I cream your cracked lips
To coax you into a smile,
Instead you stretch your lips
Into a yawn that rips
Half your face, my little one;
I must change to camomile

You take hours to feed,
And in your greed
You don't notice your other end
You have shattered
the white of my dress
with your yellow and brown mess

I bury my face in your tummy
To hear the laughter that brings me close to tears
I close your mouth to make you say mummy
But when you see your father
You confirm my worst fears
You say da-da and burst into laughter

When I went in to deliver you,
Send me a card, she said, do,
I picked Michelangelo's 'Creation of Adam'
From my old decaying stock
The gender turned out to be accurate.
But who would've thought that reality would mock
Oh, damn – the perfection of art

And now that you are almost four,
I must recount the pains, the joy
But what are these to the grief I have known
When I was told that when you are grown
You may not walk, may not talk,
That you may be a wheelchair boy.

Rahila Gupta

Baby Talk II

When he dribbles a silken thread on my sleeve,
Underlining the unbroken connections,
Below-zero weather conditions
turn the wet patch to a sheet of ice
mirroring his cross-eyed affection
I move my arm, the ice cracks
I am left with a memory of a reflection
This is how my expectation of perfection miscarried.

Rahila Gupta

Baby Talk III

Let me tell you, instead
Of a woman I met
Whose child had taken
To holding his breath
Three times over – a cot death
Surviving with dire consequences

Six months she took, to accept
That his arms and legs would not move
That drugs to contain his fits
Would splinter his sense of reality

Then, one day, she came to me and said,
Drew herself up to a grand five foot nine
But her voice spliced the air in a fine hair line,
They tell me he cannot see, cannot hear,
How will I wade through his dark silence
I held her hand but turned away
She can't afford to drown in my tears

Rahila Gupta

The Heera

Long ago in the mists of time an African Chief loved an Indian Princess. To bind her to him he gave her a Diamond of Diamonds. Hanging around her neck it sparkled into a thousand shafts of rainbow light and he said, 'The shimmer of the diamond is as nothing to the radiance of your eyes,' and he told her that the diamond contained his heart and now that she was his heart itself, she must return before the end of two years, else being so long bereft of his heart he would die.

The princess returned to her land and as she wandered among the mango groves and flower gardens of her father's house the present pushed away the past and the voice of her lover faded from her mind; while she exchanged sweet words with another the diamond flashed and grew ever more brilliant around her neck. The two years passed and on one sweet scented morning a scream shattered the dawn tranquillity. They found the princess fallen to the floor, the diamond tight against her throat, a spot of red burning within its heart . . .

Surinder cursed as her motorbike ploughed through a large puddle of old rainwater, splashing her with runny-squiggly worms of mud. Whirling through the huge iron gates she brought the bike to a smooth halt in front of the huge white house, nestling among the trees that fanned out and around it. Scanning the windows and walls her heart slipped into that old rhythm of anxiety and anger: the warring, emotional pendulum of her growing in this house. Leaning against the bike she rolled herself a cigarette, waiting for the agitation of her insides to subside.

The heavy doors swung open and an antique servant dressed in the style of the Imperial Raj stepped forward and waited, his eyes on the glowing tip of her cigarette. So Burdaji was still alive!

Refusing to acknowledge his presence, she inhaled and exhaled, mini-clouds of smoke diffusing in the air towards him. When she was ready she threw the tip over her shoulder and without a word spoken walked past him. As her back receded into the house a tongue flicked out and licked dry shrunken lips.

Deeply engrossed, Ashok sat cross-legged in front of an intricately carved bookrest, a white shawl draped over his shoulders, eyes steadily travelling across the open pages of a book. Behind him the walls were a luxurious patchwork of dusky velvety colours; books in leather, silk, metal, heavy and rich in their texture and design, lined the walls. Two golden birds flying past each other swung in perpetual suspension from the ceiling, cradling globes of light in their wings. Knowing she should slip off her boots, Surinder walked forward till she stood directly in front of Ashok.

'It's raining outside?' His pained eyes resting on the mud.

'No.'

'Did you have to go much out of your way to find the right ditch?'

'Not at all. You know this house was always my favourite ditch.' Sinking on to the cushion by the window, fingers knotting and unknotting the fringed ends of her chuni. 'Strange seeing it after such a long time. Expecting changes. But of course,' she added with a brittle smile, 'that was always my mistake.' Ashok remained silent, his eyes unrevealing. 'Hey, I've got a riddle for you. What . . .'

'Please,' Ashok held up his hand, 'must you bring your market-place manners here?'

'You're right. I shouldn't. They're too good for this place.'

'There's no change in you either. You're as perverse and arrogant as you always were.'

She shrugged her shoulders. 'I'm only what this house made me. Tell me, what's the secret of Burdaji's long life? Do you pickle him in a jar and take him out for when visitors need to be impressed by the long dynastic history of this family?'

'You never liked him, did you?'

'On the contrary. It would just irk me, a tiny bit, when he would

71

look straight through me and in his impeccable way let me know I didn't deserve to exist, in this house, in this family.'

'Burdaji was trained by the British. He has high standards.'

Surinder straightened up. 'If you really want to insult me, you'll have to do better than that.'

'The Diamond of Diamonds is gone.' His words crashed through her mind like a stone through glass and for once she was speechless, just staring at him. 'Three days ago, Burdaji unlocked the room to let in the cleaners,' Ashok continued in a detached, anecdotal voice. 'Only then did they see that the casket had been shattered and the Heera gone. There was no other sign of disturbance.'

'You've told the police?'

'We called them the next day.'

'Why so late?' she flared out at him. 'Why not immediately?'

'We had to make our own enquiries. One of the servants may have been tempted.'

'By which time it had probably been taken out of the country. Well done. Such quick thinking.'

'Anger can do nothing in this situation. However, I do appreciate your feelings at the loss of such an important family heirloom,' his cool voice pausing for an instant, 'quite apart from the fact that you were to inherit it. Did you want to possess it so badly that you couldn't wait?'

It was the disdain in his voice that stung her, not the accusation. She moved over to him till they were eye to eye. 'Just because you're a worm, don't make the mistake of imagining everyone else is, too. You may have pawned your brain to the maggots; I haven't.'

It shocked her to see the door of the Heera room ajar. For as long as she could remember, the openings and closings of that door had been attended by ritual and ceremony, always requiring the presence of several people. Stepping through the door felt like stepping through a thin slice of pain. 'Don't be so melodramatic,' she told herself crossly, her foot moving gingerly around the jagged pieces of glass on the floor, pieces of the shattered casket which had once housed the Heera.

Going over to the window, she remembered herself at a younger age; in her mind's eye saw again the young girl who would peer in from the outside: lifting herself on to the ledge, hands cupped around her eyes, nose pressed against the glass, gaze fixed in fascination on the Diamond of Diamonds, a shimmering jewel descended through the mists of time and carrying with it stories of a woman's treachery and betrayal. Ashok had discovered and denounced her obsession, ever eager to humiliate her. Sir Sunder, (father to him and uncle to her) in true *Boy's Own* style, had punished him for snitching and her for avarice. Across the years Ashok's voice came back to taunt her and tell her that the Heera was a symbol of woman's corruption and therefore it would suit her well: Surinder-the-illegitimate, Surinder-the-unwanted, Surinder-the-charity-case.

As diverse as the stories of the Heera's history, so similarly maze-like were the stories of her birth. Her father, the family vagabond, had brought to his brother's house, Sir Sunder's house, a baby girl; his daughter, he said. Of the mother he would say nothing, or everything depending on the ratio of alcohol to blood in his body; with each telling the story became a variegated wonder, where truth and fiction joined hands to confuse, confess, and/or obliterate. Who knows? One thing her father did obtain, for her good, he thought, and for which she should be ever grateful, others declared, was Sir Sunder's promise that she would be accepted eldest daughter of the family.

A whisper of a movement snapped her out of her memories, and turning around from the window she saw Burdaji standing by the door; his body language said he'd been waiting patiently for her to notice him and be escorted out. Surinder smiled. It was good that Burdaji would never change, particularly in his attitude towards her. One needed some certainties in this world.

Space hogs! Not even enough room in between the cars for her to park her bike. This place was too fast becoming a yuppie ghetto. Parking around the corner and rushing back to the flat, hoping her friends hadn't come and gone. No one waiting at the door. She'd missed them. Now she'd have to spend half the evening on the

73

phone apologising all round. Opening the door, her hand trailed over the wall to flick on the lightswitch and stayed there. Light flooded a room in which chairs and tables had been overturned, books torn and scattered on the floor, cushions ripped open, her precious paintings torn from their hangings . . . She hadn't thought of it but her body must have been ready, startled into nervous anticipation by the room's devastation, ready to kick back, pull the hand about to clamp on her mouth, to half turn, lever with her hips and throw him groaning on to the floor where his plump body bounced like a rubber ball, to quickly sit on his back and pin his arms across his shoulders till he cried out in agony.

'Who are you? What are you doing here?'

'Nothing, I wasn't doing anything.'

'Why did you wreck my home?' Giving his arms another twist and smiling with grim satisfaction at his yell.

'Ooooh! You'll break my arms. Can't breathe. All right, all right. I'll tell,' as he felt the impending pain of another twist. 'Let go first.'

'Tell first.'

'I'm a very simple man.'

Pretty obvious, she wanted to say, but kept her thoughts to herself, not wanting to break his concentration.

'I'm an ordinary burglar bloke; doing your place over, I was. Now let go.' Plump body heaving, trying to break free, breath coming in laboured gasps.

'You need to lose some weight. Did you know I'm a solicitor?' His despairing groan said no. 'Being in that line of work, I know a little bit about burglars. One thing they don't do is hang around for the owners to come back. They reckon it's bad for business.' She bent down to whisper into his ear. 'Were you looking for something?'

'Told you. I'm just a burglar.'

'Tell me another one.' Taking her chuni and lifting his arms even higher, she tied them together; good thing this dupatta was made of strong material. Moving towards his legs she tied them together with a belt and then stood back to survey her handiwork. Rubber Ball thrashed up and down like a stranded whale.

'It'll be bad for you if you don't let me go. My friends will be along soon, and they won't be dainty with you neither. Not like me.'

'Threatening now!' She picked up the phone. Alarm spread over Rubber Ball like a tidal wave.

'What are you doing? Who're you calling? Let me go. I'll do a deal with you.'

She gave him a cup of coffee and let him go. She couldn't decide if his surprise had been greatest at the coffee or the prospect of freedom as she held the door open for him. He didn't know much. They had been hired by a man called Tierney to search her flat for the Heera; failing to discover the desired property they'd left Rubber Ball behind to wait for her; they'd made the fatal mistake of trusting a stereotype and had thought that one man would be sufficient to overpower a passive little Asian woman and drag the truth out of her.

It was late in the night and sleep refused to come as the shadow of the Heera danced through her thoughts, a useless hunk of stone whose only worth lay in delighting the eye and whose very existence said to the world, I am proof of woman's treachery and betrayal. Through the centuries the truth of the Heera had been lost and that which remained, the story of a princess who had callously deceived a lover, had been told and retold with growing relish; the passing of time had added further stories of the women who had worn the Heera, and of the pain and suffering that had followed in their wake.

At first she thought the urgent ringing was a part of her dream, but its persistence dragged her into full consciousness. Wondering if her visitors had decided to return, she grabbed the kirpan her father had left her. Kirpan held at the ready, she opened the door with a quick swing and almost fell flat as Ashok lurched forward, body shaking, his clothes and face blood-stained. Dropping the kirpan, she helped him to a chair.

'Get the Heera.' His voice hoarse and strained.

Anger sparked within her. 'Damn you! I wouldn't take that stupid piece of rock if you doubled it and offered it to me on your precious bended knees.'

Ashok's old mocking smile flitted across his battered face. 'Get off your high horse, and listen. I know what happened to it, but you have to go and get it. You're going to love this. Apparently Burdaji decided you weren't good enough to inherit the Heera, plus that our dwindling fortunes needed a boost. So he sold it.' She opened her mouth and then closed it, without having said a syllable. 'Don't get me wrong. It wasn't a normal sell; it couldn't be. The Heera was to be removed from the house in a fake steal. That way the family coffers would get the payment for the Heera, as well as the insurance money for its theft, and no one the wiser that Burdaji was at the bottom of it. I must say I'm impressed. Neat.'

'Stinks.'

'However, plans went rather awry. Before the fake steal could happen, there was a real steal. These bruises assure me of that. Burdaji, to borrow from your vocabulary, is in the shithouse. He didn't have time to tell me much before they hustled him off, but there's someone called the Chief, who was also interested. That's the only lead we've got, and we haven't got much time either. The Heera is the ransom for Burdaji's release. They haven't given us much time.'

'I'm terribly busy at the moment. Overworked, underpaid; you know how it is . . .'

Abandoning her usual shalwar/kameez, Surinder dug out one of the more elaborate saris Sir Sunder had dutifully bought for her, heavy gold patterns balanced on a greeen that shivered into different shades as the light slithered over its folds and pleats. Throwing the end over her shoulder so that it dangled heavy and long towards the floor, she stood for a sober moment trying to recognise the woman who stared back at her from the mirror, whose upswept hair and glinting jewellery made her a stranger to herself. If this was the effect of a few ordinary ornaments, what devastating transformation could the Heera wreak?

The Chief's house was way out in the country, and set way back from the road, behind thick trees and in the middle of what seemed to be an open zoo. Surinder parked Ashok's car only inches away from a lion and his mate. They stared at her and she stared back, trying to control her fear, her feet sticking to the ground. A touch on her arm awoke her awareness and a smiling face indicated the open door. Gulping and looking over her shoulder, she followed the maid inside.

They lounged in the back garden while the servants brought out tea, cakes, biscuits and fruit. The Chief talked of the animals that roamed his gardens, living mementoes of the African home he missed so much. Surinder agreed that it was reassuring to have with one dear mementoes of one's home in this foreign country and told him how she had been searching for a little piece of rock that was precious to her and had been lost, and of how dearly she would love to have it back because it was as valuable as life to her; and, she added looking out across the garden, that no price would be too great to pay to regain that precious memento. The Chief was full of sympathy and commiseration. He recounted how his country had also lost a very beautiful, precious treasure; a foolish man, blinded by love, had given it away to a treacherous woman. Surinder, her hand playing with the gold chain around her throat, admitted that she had heard a similar story, but since it had happened centuries ago how could anyone know whether it was true or not. The Chief's voice was as polite as ever, though now it contained a steely, unyielding quality.

'We know what is true, and we only desire that which once was ours. It must return to the home it came from before it was so deceitfully removed. Certain things can never be for sale.'

And so it had ended and so she was thinking and waiting, ruminating on what had gone and what she should be doing. Parked a little way from the gates of the Chief's house, she sat behind the wheel, nibbling at her knuckles, knowing there was no going back without the Heera. Such feebleness would earn her her own contempt, let alone Ashok's. She could hardly hoof it through the gardens with those friendly pets roaming around; entry would have to be effected in some other manner. Time passed, she counted the leaves on the trees, the grass blades on the verge, the birds in the sky, the birds in her brain, decided she was distinctly batty, when the sight of a small van coming towards her, the Chief's crest

77

emblazoned on the bonnet, made her sit up, smarten up and step out. She hailed the driver and, as he slowed, ran towards him in what she hoped were dainty and feminine steps; flashing him her sincerest maiden-in-distress smile she asked him if he would look at her car as it just wouldn't go and she supposed there must be something wrong with the engine but, oh dear, she didn't know a thing about these things, etc, etc. The young driver was most obliging. He got out, lifted the hood of the car and bent forward to peer into the engine's intestines. That was when she conked him.

Dragging him into the car, she took off his clothes, dressed herself in them, wrapped her sari tight around him; his resemblance to an Egyptian mummy wasn't far off! Holding the kirpan at his throat, her hand swung round his face in a couple of hard, sharp slaps. The poor man blinked, looked as if he didn't know where on earth he was, saw her in his clothes, saw the kirpan at his throat and, deciding that unconsciousness was the most blessed state of all, carefully closed his eyes again. Surinder prodded him gently with the kirpan, then not so gently; his eyes remained closed. Keeping up the pressure; the thin line of skin was about to break when he gave a little choking sound and his eyes flew open.

'Don't look so worried!' in her most reassuring voice. 'Your clothes look rather nifty on me, don't you think? But, as you are probably thinking, and quite rightly, no one goes to this trouble just 'cos they hate shopping. Give me a tiny piece of information and I'll leave you in peace. Honest. You can trust me. Just tell me, whisper it in my ear if you like, tell me where the Diamond of Diamonds is kept? In which room and the security around it.' He didn't like the question; that was obvious because he tried his old trick of pretending to be unconscious again. The kirpan dug in again. 'Look, I know life is hard, and I wish we could all sleep through it, too. You'd better tell me what I want to know or . . .' The kirpan broke the skin barrier and spots of blood welled up.

Suddenly his eyes swung open and faced her almost gloatingly. 'I'll tell you. But you won't be able to get it because I don't think you have that kind of courage or foolishness.'

'Oh, Mother,' thought Surinder, 'he was right. Dead right.' The Heera lay in a glass box which lay in another, bigger glass box, and in between the two coiled an undulating live, lethal snake. 'Damn Burdaji,' she cursed. 'Damn, damn, damn.' Back rigid against the wall, fighting the nausea rising in her throat, eyes looking everywhere but at that thing! If there was anything she couldn't stand, if there was one thing she hated, it was/it is: SNAKES!

She would give up and go with honour. She'd already done more than duty demanded. Getting the uniform had been a brilliant idea, slipping into the house and locating the right room had been downright clever, conking out the guard at the door, in her best conking out manner, had been a crowning finale to the day's achievements. She opened the door to go out, the kirpan clanking against the doorpost. It was made of good strong material, she'd used it for all sorts of hacking jobs round the flat. Swinging round before she could think another thought, she lifted it high and struck with all her strength, hoping to catch IT in its downward passage; IT's tail was sliced off, but the main body leapt towards her, hood stretched out in menace. Desperately she slashed out, weaving the kirpan in front of her. Cut into pieces, IT fell away. Her legs buckled in relief. Perhaps she'd better start believing in God. Her hand closed over the Heera and slipped it into her pocket.

Shots rang out and in the mirror she saw men and dogs running after her; her foot pushed the accelerator to the floor as the van hurtled out through the gates and on to the road. She was a little safer. The Chief could hardly call the police.

Evening came down like a tattered curtain, obscuring the shapes of buildings, turning the dereliction of this abandoned council estate into an obstacle course of hidden traps. Keeping close to the walls she searched for Sunflower House, the rendezvous point. Stumbling against a block of concrete she almost banged her head against the sign and sighed in irritation. The obvious was always under one's nose. Moving along the corridors she found that half the flats weren't even numbered; vandals are so inconsiderate! Flat 59 didn't have a number, either, and as no light or sound came from it, she wondered if Tierney was playing a hoax on them. Just then she heard the sound of a door bang inside the flat, a murmur of voices and footsteps coming towards the front door. She slipped back to the stairs. As the man passed her she stepped out and dug her faithful kirpan into his back.

'Quiet,' she warned, 'or you'll find your clothes need a little mending,' her mind trying to remember which movie that line came from. 'Who's in the flat?'

'No one. Only me. It's empty.' Something about the voice clicked in her memory. She took out her lighter and flicked it on. 'Turn around.'

'Jesus Christ!' exclaimed Rubber Ball in astonishment.

'No. Just little ol' me. Thought you were going to leave this business.'

'I'm trying, ain't I? Not easy to slip away from a life of unbridled crime and become a respectable citizen. Takes time. What are you doing here?'

'Nothing much. Thought I'd rescue the old man.'

'What!' Rubber Ball was shocked into a shout. Clamping a hand round his mouth, he peered along the corridor to see if anyone had heard and come out. 'Look, love. Me, I'm gentle as a lamb. Me, you can tackle any day. Tierney, he is a nasty piece of work. And vicious. Mustn't forget that. Take my advice, go back home and send a few of your male friends round.'

'Can't. Could do with some of your male help. Will you?'

On noiseless feet she slipped into the flat and through towards the back room. Peering through a crack she saw Burdaji sitting stiff and straight on a decrepit old bed in the corner, his uniform rumpled, untidy and awry, his shoulders sagging, empty of his habitual arrogance and authority. Burdaji's face moved from side to side following the flying movement of something winging across the room to land on the wall opposite with a dull thud, another followed and another and a voice out of her sight cursed in frustration. A man's figure, she guessed to be Tierney, crossed her vision and then re-crossed, his eyes on his hands, sorting out a bunch of darts.

Having had Burdaji to instil her with a perfect set of manners she knocked on the door to announce her presence and, smiling pleasantly, stepped forward. 'Hello. Not too early, am I? You must be Tierney? How do you do,' hand outstretched to shake his. You

80

could see Tierney hadn't been brought up proper; he stepped back and pulled out a gun.

'Who you?' he growled.

'What's happened to the young master?' Burdaji asked, getting up shakily and as usual purely concerned about his own priorities.

'Apart from a few cracked ribs, external bruising, internal pains, he's all right. I'm Ashok's cousin,' she said, turning to Tierney. 'He asked me to convey his apologies, but as you may have gathered, he's rather indisposed and asked me to come in his place. You don't mind, do you?'

'Where's the diamond?' Tierney didn't waste time in getting to the point.

'Let him go and you can have it.'

'Diamond first.'

'Him first.'

Tierney pulled Burdaji towards him. 'Hand over the diamond, woman, or this senile old git is going to be packed off to his happy hunting home in the sky. Get it?'

She got it. Tierney had watched too many westerns. With a sigh she reached into her bag and brought out a small heavily wrapped packet. As Tierney reached for it he suddenly grunted in pain, a dart sticking into his side; surprise flipped to anger as he turned towards Burdaji, the gun arching out towards Burdaji's head. Surinder moved, her leg kicking the gun from his hand and her elbow smashing across his chin.

'Quick. Get out,' she turned and hissed to Burdaji; before he could reply she found herself hitting the floor as Tierney swung at her from the back and a boot crunched across her head. In a haze of pain her fingers clawed at the ankle, digging into the flesh and twisted the foot sharply to one side.

'Fucking bitch,' Tierney said over and over again as he almost lost his balance before grappling her back to the floor, his knees pinning her down and a dart teasing backwards and forwards across her face. 'Now where shall I start? Those big brown eyes? An ear, nose and throat job? No. Let's start on these nice tender cheeks.' A shot rang out and Tierney's body collapsed on her. The gun dropped from Burdaji's shaking hands.

'Yuck,' exclaimed Surinder, shoving the lifeless body away from her, determined not to look, feeling slimy with his blood, teeth and lips tight clenched against the nausea that rose in her throat. Struggling up she pulled Burdaji to the door.

'We can't,' Burdaji protested. 'His men will be here by now. They'll catch us outside.'

'Don't think so.' Hustling Burdaji out, mouth opening and closing, gulping in the fresh night air, like an alki at closing time. 'I've got a suspicion his men received some garbled message and they perhaps ended up at the wrong address.' This day was full of surprises; for the first time in her life she saw Burdaji chuckling and laughing. 'But just in case, let's leg it, and besides, I've got a tense, nervous headache.'

'It's criminal.' The man was outraged and offended.

'If you won't do it, I'll just take it somewhere else,' Surinder replied. With tenderness and awe he picked up the Heera and cradled it in his palm, moving it round, turning it different ways. 'I had heard of it, of course, and the legends that go with it. Madam, how could you want this destroyed?'

She took the Heera from his hand and held it in her own. Even though she'd decided to relinquish it, it still belonged to her and she wanted it for as long as she could have it.

'Let's say I want to recycle it.' The man flinched at the word.

'Why have it cut into tiny pieces? It's worth far more as a whole.'

'It's too dangerous as one, whole, piece. It's a flame for women to burn in. Will you do it?'

She had told Ashok she didn't want it but Burdaji had insisted on passing it on to her in a little ceremony at the house, saying he should not have tried to go against tradition. The new mellowness in his voice churned up all the old feelings inside her into a chaotic mess. Dammit. She much preferred the old astringent Burdaji. You knew where you were with him. The Heera was now hers, to do with as she pleased, to wear or beware. For the last time she looked into its brilliant, glinting heart. Was there really a spot of red in the middle, or was it her imagination? Closing her hand over it, she turned the fist around and put it on the table. Unlocking her fingers and lifting her hand away, she said, 'The cheque should go to the African Women's Organisation. I've given you the address.'

She watched him walk over to his workbench, place the Heera in a dop to hold it tight and switch on the saw. As the saw cut into it she thought she heard the mocking laughter of the Princess telling her she was a fool.

Ravinder Randhawa

The Spell and the Ever-Changing Moon

       Nisa looked around nervously as she walked along the dusty edge of the road on that suffocating July afternoon. She was in a part of Lahore which she did not know very well but all the landmarks her neighbour Apa Zarina had described had been appearing so far. She tugged at the burqa round her shoulders as if afraid of being recognised through its thin georgette veil and the black silky folds that cloaked her neat, compact little figure. It belonged to her unmarried friend Seema and had been borrowed specially for the occasion. It was the first time in her life that she had embarked on a mission aware that it wasn't 'permitted'. She was trembling a little with guilt and fear. Her breathing and heartbeat quickened as she approached the house.

Just as Zarina had said, it stood at the end of the *kutchi abaadi*. A small house, one of the few here which were brick built. Right outside its entrance was the lean-to of the motorbike repair shop which she was told to look out for. Two men sat there tinkering with motorbikes which looked too rusty and battered to be repaired. They looked up from their sweaty labour each time a woman went in or out of the green door of Talat's house.

Most of the women who came had their faces covered with shawls or dupattas and some, like Nisa, wore burqas. But occasionally the men succeeded in catching a glimpse of a young and fresh female face. In any case they weren't discouraged by the veils and cloaks. If the outline or gait indicated a youngish woman they did their best to draw attention by shouting a veiled obscenity or by humming a snatch of a film song.

The women had been trained for years to sidestep and ignore this kind of behaviour. So they all scurried past, hastening their footsteps just a little. Nisa, who was skilled in the same strategy, quickened her pace to reach the shelter of the house although she had been fearful of the ultimate step she was going to take. It was for her a house of Evil.

She stood looking around the bare courtyard for a second. In one corner was the usual outside tap in its sunken cemented square used for washing. Across the length of the courtyard hung the laundry drying at the remarkable speed which only the brilliant afternoon sun made possible. She hesitated for an instant and then walked into the small room beyond.

Her eyes were blinded by the sudden fragrant darkness of the room and she steadied herself against the door jamb as she stumbled over the stock of shoes near the door. Slipping off hers, Nisa sat down just inside the doorway. She gasped as her eyes began to see.

Talat sat on a low stage with two huge black snakes entwined round her body. She was dramatically good-looking and very fashionable. Her large black eyes were highlighted by the blackest kohl and her small delicate mouth was painted a brilliant red, matching the nail varnish on her carefully manicured hands. Through her fine black lawn kurta was clearly outlined a shapely bosom and a slender waist. She was muttering to herself, eyes closed, body swaying rhythmically, whilst the women round her stared in hypnotised fascination.

Nisa's glance surveyed the room quickly. The sunlight had been shut out. In the dim lamplight she could make out crudely painted pictures of holy faces which she had never seen before. She remembered hearing about distant foreign lands where it was customary to paint portraits of saints, a practice she knew was definitely blasphemous, and she hastily touched her ears inwardly in a gesture of pardon. '*Tauba, tauba*', she sought forgiveness. In one corner burned scented candles emitting whitish clouds of smoke with a cloying sweet smell. On the mantelshelf stood a photo of Talat with her 'guru' who looked remarkably young and healthy as he smiled down at her with his hand resting on her head in benediction.

The queue was moving slowly. People were leaving one by one

as each managed to get a personal audience with Talat. There was the usual assortment of problems: mother-in-law or daughter-in-law ones, there were patients seeking cures for incurable diseases, the destitute looking for a better future. Whatever their problems, Talat gave them that hope they knew they did not have.

No one seemed to have come alone except Nisa. She trembled again. It would be her turn soon to speak to Talat. She wasn't sure even now what she would say or what she would ask for. She held her cheap plastic handbag in a fierce clutch under her left arm and in her right hand she held a brown paper bag containing the four eggs she had bought on her way up, according to Zarina's instructions. The sweat from her fingers had formed a damp, dark ring round the base of the paper bag. She wondered uncomfortably if it was going to give way.

As the crowd in the room thinned, Nisa found herself slowly moving nearer to the raised dais. Within half an hour she was face to face with Talat. Nisa looked up into the dark, warm, liquid eyes. Disconcerted by Talat's youthful appearance, she felt for an instant she had made a mistake. Talat's eyes smiled as if they'd read her thoughts.

'How can I help you, my daughter?' she asked, as if a little amused by this belated scepticism. Her manner and her address claimed for herself the supremacy and status which age automatically bestows on everyone in that world, a manner which seemed strangely inappropriate in someone who was perhaps only nineteen or twenty.

But Nisa was overwhelmed by the encouraging sympathy and affection in her voice and felt the tears welling up in her throat. She could only say, 'It's my husband . . .' before she broke down into a fit of sobbing, aware that she was being stared at very curiously. This kind of desperation was always useful as it impressed other clients. Talat soothed her gently and tenderly.

'Hush, my daughter, have faith. I can help you.' Her voice was reassuring. She eyed the bag in Nisa's hands and asked in a whisper, 'Do you want me to do a *chowkie* for you?' Nisa could only nod an affirmative. Talat proceeded quickly to perform that ritual. She relieved Nisa of the eggs and placed them in a neat square on a small wooden stool. Nisa stopped crying as she watched in fascination. Talat's fingers moved dextrously as she placed a bowl beside the stool and then began to unwind the snakes from her body. She pulled both of them up to the eggs and closed her eyes, rocking forwards and backwards as if in a trance.

Nisa's body stiffened with fear as the snakes stood dangerously close to her for a few seconds, sniffing the eggs and then raising their heads in what looked like vicious contempt. There was absolute silence in the room as everyone watched. Talat came out of her trance and her assistant, a very plain woman of around thirty-five or so, helped her to capture the snakes and put them away in two large colourful wicker baskets.

The snakes slithered and hissed as if in protest, but were soon put away. While the other woman was covering the baskets with pieces of black cloth, Talat began to break the eggs one by one into the clay bowl. Nisa tried to watch her but felt compelled to watch the snakes.

Suddenly she heard Talat's voice cursing under her breath and looked fearfully down at the bowl. On top of the cracked eggs floated nails, blood and some strange, noxious and ugly greenish matter.

'Ah, my daughter,' Talat exclaimed as she folded her hands and closed her eyes as if to seek help from above. Nisa shuddered and covered her face with both hands in shock and horror.

'You are deep in difficulties, I can see.' Talat was shaking her head in concern. 'You need the Art to help you. You can change the path of your man, you know. There is a way . . .'

The pitch of her voice had changed. Nisa was shivering visibly now. Talat had come out of her trance and leaned closer to Nisa. She whispered confidentially in her ears as the other women stared. Nisa had kept the lower half of her veil stretched across her face but the curious audience could see her anxious brown eyes widen with horror as they hung on Talat's face, drinking in her whispered words.

She felt dumbfounded and shaken. With her finger on the clasp of her handbag she looked at Talat's companion and began fumblingly, 'What's the . . . the fee? What shall I . . .?'

The woman glanced at Talat's face and replied gushingly, 'Oh, there's no fee really, Bibi. But we do have to take some *nazars* for the snakes, you know. It's ten rupees for the *chowkie*, Bibi. And,' she continued again quickly, 'you know Talat Bibi has to draw a *chilla* many times to get her powers. That's very very hard work, Bibi. And you need *nazars* for the snakes, you know, Bibi. It's twenty-five rupees in all.'

She was observing Nisa closely as she spoke, the changing expression in Nisa's eyes guiding her in her reckoning of the bill. Nisa pushed the greasy notes with clumsy and clammy fingers into the assistant's eager hands and stumbled to her feet hastily.

Outside, she tripped over the burning stones in the paved courtyard and then on the threshold of the green door. The two men looked up and jeered again but Nisa neither saw nor heard them. She was too preoccupied with those strange whispered words. She saw the bus approaching from the right direction and ran towards it, relieved at not having to wait in the blistering heat near that evil place.

In all her twenty-six years she had never been so shocked by what she had heard or seen. Neither the shock years ago, of seeing some pornographic pictures that a girl at school had found in her father's trunk; nor that other time when she had woken up in the middle of the night as the family slept on the rooftop and suddenly realised that the neighbours were actually 'doing it' could compare. She had blushed into the pillow and covered her ears to block out the muffled sounds. The mental picture of Chachi Nuggo's massive breasts flashed in her mind and the thought of Chachaji on top of her embarrassed her even as she remembered it now, almost ten years later.

'It's indecent even to think of it,' she reprimanded herself. Her mind returned again to the present and tried to grapple with what Talat had just told her.

'Women,' she'd said, 'are powerful beings. If you want your man to be utterly in your power all you have to do is to give him a drop of your own blood to drink.' As Nisa stared at Talat, vaguely apprehensive, she elaborated her meaning. 'Menstrual blood has great magical powers, you know. A man can never overcome the

88

spell. He will become a slave to your will.'

Nisa shuddered again as she remembered the words with horror and revulsion. The very thought seemed so impure to her, so unclean. She felt certain that the knowledge came from the devil. 'I couldn't do such an awful thing, even to Hameed,' she mused to herself, wondering longingly for a few seconds about how it would feel if Hameed was indeed a slave to her will. She tried determinedly to shake off the idea.

'Ammah was right,' she thought. 'Never to go to these weird places. They are truly evil . . . There can be no doubt about it.'

She really regretted having gone to see Talat. If it hadn't been for Zarina she'd never have done it. 'No one really believes in these things these days,' she thought. 'Yet Zarina's mother does look so much better now.' The justification for the trip also rose from within her heart.

The debate continued in her mind all the way back through town on the bus. It was almost time for Asar prayers; the shadows had doubled in length, she noticed, as she got off near the Mini Market and walked round the shops to the row of poky little houses behind them. Her footsteps quickened as she thought of the children being looked after by Zarina.

Her neighbour was full of questions but Nisa could not bring herself to repeat what Talat had told her. She just hedged round the questions and rushed off with her brood, saying she still had the dinner to cook.

She fed the older children and sat down to nurse the youngest of her two boys, Zafar. Her mind was still occupied by her afternoon's adventure. She now felt curiously subdued and guilty about it. Zarina had meant well. In fact Nisa often felt guilty even about the fact that her neighbours knew the problems she was having with her marriage.

Her mother had always stressed the dignity and value of reserve. 'A good woman,' she used to say, 'knows how to keep the family's secrets. What's the use, anyway, of telling people seven doors away that your month's allowance hasn't quite stretched to the last four days this month? If possible you manage to survive without letting the world know.'

Nisa felt that was indeed where she'd failed to act as a really good wife. Her neighbours on all three sides of her knew her dark secret. Her own family did not know. She was proud of that. Every time someone had come to visit her from her home town, Sialkot, she had kept up appearances quite well. But she hadn't been able to hide the truth from her neighbours.

Each night when Hameed got home, looking drunk and forbidding, she strengthened her resolve to keep out of his way and not to cause a row, but five nights out of ten she failed. He seemed to seek her out as if that was what he'd been waiting for all day. She wished sometimes that he could come home earlier so that the noise of his rowing would be less noticeable. At eleven the whole neighbourhood was quiet and each abusive mouthful he hurled at her could be heard at least three doors away. Sometimes there were flying plates and howling children, if they happened to wake up. A couple of times she had lost control herself and had begun to scream hysterically with fear.

Anyway she realised that it had got easier for her since the neighbours knew. Sometimes when the row was a really bad one Zarina would call out to ask if she was all right. The shame of that always got through to Hameed, even if he was really drunk, and it made him stop and go to bed grumbling about interfering busybody neighbours.

His anger and abuse was often followed by an overbearingly vicious assertion of his conjugal rights which Nisa never dared to deny him, and she believed she ought not to dare to deny him either. She never resisted him but she resented his heavy-handed impatience. She hated the stink of cheap home-brewed beer on his breath with all the moral weight of her mother's censure of drinking. And she missed the snatches of wooing from the early days of her marriage.

After the day's wearying labour, it was that physical humiliation borne in silence five nights out of ten which was consuming her. She loathed that physical submission to his will. It had to be done like the housework and the caring of the children. It was her part of the deal, her return for the housekeeping allowance. She didn't argue about that but she bitterly resented his drinking. Though she

wouldn't dare argue with him, she was unable to conceal her
disapproval. And her tight-lipped hostility aggravated his bad
temper. He was riled by her strong sense of moral superiority into
an even deeper viciousness. Sometimes this worked for her. He
would be too angry to want her afterwards. Sometimes he would
be too drunk to notice her aloofness or her lofty anger and he just
pleased himself

That evening as she lay on her charpoy in the courtyard staring
at the clear night sky, a vision of Talat's face kept intruding into her
thoughts. It was a picture of Talat which compelled her imagination. She saw her standing waist-deep in the shallower waters of
the Ravi, dressed in black, eyes uplifted to the moon, invoking her
powers. Power, the very thought of power, seemed so seductive to
Nisa in her helpless situation. She had been adventurous that
morning but she knew she couldn't be as brave as Talat, though she
longed to have some control over her circumstances.

She jumped up as she heard Hameed's footsteps at the door. It
was nearly eleven, his usual time. She quickly raised the simmering
water on the stove to the boil and tipped the rice in. That night as
Hameed launched into his usual nagging and complaining between
each morsel of curried lentils and rice, Nisa felt her resolve to
never think about magic weakening.

She wondered how much pain it took, how much courage, to
pollute a man's cup of tea or glass of sherbet. She watched Hameed's
lips pressed against the glass of water and shivered. Through her
mind flashed a memory of her first-born Karim, newly arrived,
lying across her belly, sticky and a little blood-stained. She had
touched him unbelievingly . . . the sight of the drops of blood on the
cord hadn't really worried her or repulsed her then. That was the
clot of blood that had made him possible, given him life.

'What are you staring at?' Hameed snapped peevishly, and Nisa
jumped to her feet again to clear up the plates. Somewhere in the
recesses of her mind she had caught a glimpse of herself performing
a grossly sacrilegious spell and that glimpse had unnerved her for a
few seconds.

All her life she had seen the women around her observing the
taboos as far as this area of their lives was concerned. Nisa herself

had developed a deep sense of shame over the years through the secrecy and the avoidances. Now it was as though Talat had pulled out a vital brick at the base of that belief.

If it really had magical powers, why did women abhor it so, she wondered. She knew she was too simple to work out the answers but the question rose insistently within her heart each month when she menstruated. The abhorrence didn't make sense to her now that she thought about it. After all, they all knew enough about the physical aspect of menstruation. Wasn't there some mild relief when girls 'started' or worry when they were 'late'?

Seven months passed by with the creeping pace of a prison sentence. Each month she wondered if she would dare. Each month when the moon was full she remembered Talat's eyes, her face aglow in the moonlight, standing waist-deep in the waters of the Ravi, and each month the spell seemed less shocking. She thought about herself, her life and her body a great deal in those months. Each time she saw the moon she prayed for a better month, but things did not change. Except for her own attitude to her own body. That changed subtly.

Towards the end of the month, when the money began to run out on the twenty-fifth or thereabouts, a deep bitterness filled her heart. She had to turn to him again to ask him for more and have him spit in her face. They'd always been the worst nights of the month, when his anger had a sharper, more righteous edge to it. But now when that happened she resented him as deeply as he resented the increased expenses.

She had grown weary of her life. The skimping and the managing, the hard work and the violence and finally the humiliating abuse of her body. She began to refuse him. That was the way of wayward women, she'd been taught, but she no longer cared.

Hameed was nonplussed by her refusal, too surprised and hurt to argue or insist at first. But then she began to reject him more frequently and he had to react. Surprisingly, he did not take her forcibly, but became more violent in other ways. It was almost as if he was aware of her newly found veneration for her own body, and *had* to violate her in some other way.

For Nisa those refusals became a small triumph each time. The black eyes, the swollen lips or bruised face became more commonplace for her. Zarina's mother would shake her head sadly sometimes and say, 'Oh, that man, Beti. God will reward you for your patience. What makes him so angry?'

For Nisa the bruises became an option she preferred to humiliating sex. She wasn't sure that she wanted rewards in heaven; she only wished she had to suffer less on earth.

That spring Zarina's mother became ill again. The doctor came but the old lady was not reassured. She kept talking of Talat and how well her remedy had worked the year before. Nisa came back from their house with her head full of memories of the day she had gone to see Talat.

Talat was no longer an evil practitioner of magic for her. She appeared in her memory as someone gentle and loving, a friend and a sympathiser, who cared for the underdog, for her. The knowledge that Talat had imparted to her of the strange sinful spell had given her a sense of strength. Nisa had changed from being a shivering, huddled creature into a calmer and pensive woman.

That evening was women's night out. Seema was getting married the next day. They were all getting together to assemble her clothes for her trousseau, ready to be shown to the in-laws the following day. Nisa had found the right moment to obtain Hameed's permission to attend. She went round early, dressed in glittering clothes, her best earrings swinging from her ears, Zafar in her arms and the older two trailing by her side.

The girls were in high spirits, the singing was buoyant and loud. Nisa tried hard to blend into the scene but her laughter was laboured. The same old familiar well-loved tunes were jarringly painful today. The lies they told of marital bliss, of loving husbands and contented days irritated her. Nisa looked round at the little house sadly and remembered her mother's house. She was pulled out of her nostalgia by the sound of Seema's aunt lecturing her on how to cope with her new life. Forbearance and forgiveness were the operative words. That too was all too familiar.

Nisa could restrain herself no longer. She suddenly erupted, 'And how much exactly is she really supposed to endure, Chachi?

93

How many tears does it take to make a home?' She asked quietly, 'If Seema was really drowning in her own tears and being choked by her own screams, would you still not want her to look backwards at this house?'

Looking a little discomfited and annoyed, the aunt said, 'Heaven forbid, an inauspicious question for tonight, isn't it?'

Other women around them showed an interest in the conversation. Most of them knew about Nisa. Suddenly Nisa felt an arm around her shoulders. It was Seema's mother. The pain beneath the question had communicated itself to her. 'No mother could shut her doors behind her daughter forever. If Seema needed help, I would gladly let her in, of course.'

Nisa smiled with difficulty and returned to the kitchen for another teapot. Zarina was assisting in the kitchen.

'You know what?' she chirped as she saw Nisa coming in. 'I went today to Talat's house to get Ammah's medicine and I found to my great surprise that Talat and her family have disappeared.'

'What do you mean?'

'Well, packed up and shot off into the night.'

'And why?' Nisa's heart was throbbing.

'Well! The motorcycle mechanic said they had to flit because too many people kept returning to demand their money back. It seems she was a fraud.'

Nisa was quiet as she walked the short distance back home with Zarina. The children were exhausted. She took their shoes off one by one and then went into the kitchen to cook the rice, still wondering about Talat. At times she could have sworn that she actually felt the power of the magic, the spell she carried within her body. Now she felt lost and bereft again. She kept hoping that the spell she knew about was genuine.

Hameed came in later and more drunk than usual. He attacked her more viciously than usual, taunting her about her finery and the earrings. Nisa, overwrought and frightened, got up hurriedly to leave the room but he pulled her by the arm. She lost her balance, stumbled and fell to the floor. Her head hit the corner of the wooden *chowkie* and began to bleed furiously. There was a terrible clang as enamelled mugs, plates and bowls rolled off the kitchen shelf. The noise shook Hameed. He pulled himself up and tried to help Nisa up.

But she was hysterical. 'No! No! No!' she was screaming. 'Don't touch me! Don't come near me. I'll kill you. I'll stab you. I'll poison you.' Words poured out of her as fast as the blood sprang from her wound. She looked strange in her glittering clothes, blood-stained face and dishevelled hair.

Zarina was knocking on the door furiously. Hameed, bemused and shaken, let her in and went out again himself. At once Zarina took charge. She nursed Nisa's injuries, calmed her down and helped her to bed. The children had slept through the commotion.

The next morning when Nisa woke up everything was quite clear in her head. She knew what she had to do. She packed some things for herself and Zafar in a small steel trunk. The older children were at school. They walked up and came back with Zarina's children. She stood on a small stool near the wall and called Zarina to tell her.

'I'm going to my mother's house, Apa,' she said. 'I'm taking Zafar with me. I think they will not turn us away. If nothing else, I can wash dishes and cook. If Hameed cannot keep Safia and Karim let him dump them in Sialkot as well.'

Zarina nodded tearfully and promised to keep an eye on them for her. For once she did not have the courage to persuade Nisa that she must endure and that he would change. She didn't know of a magic which worked. Nisa had seen a vision she could not forget, she'd felt a power she could not deny. As she turned away and walked out of the courtyard, clutching both Zafar and the silver trunk, her steps were laboriously slow but firm and determined.

Rukhsana Ahmad

The Traveller

When, hundreds of moons ago, I slithered feet-first into this world, two tiny blue legs already kicking away the cord that bound me to my mother's womb, it was accepted by all present that I should become a traveller. In those far-off days in my almost-forgotten land, to be both a traveller and a woman was not considered a paradox. At one month of age, my mother began singing to me the songs of motion and movement taught to her by her mother. Into the perfect shells of my infant ears she poured out pictures in music, tales of people and landscapes so unlike our own, conjured up and coloured in through the light and shade of her complex rhythms and melodies.

At six months of age I could walk and climb, my feet seduced into premature agility, propelled by the growing wanderlust of my desires. At one year of age, as is our custom, all the women from our settlement were summoned to witness my naming ceremony. I was too heavy-eyed and drowsy with milk to remember the finer details, but Big Dadima still recalls the activity and excitement of that day when gradually, one by one, like galleons in full sail crossing the orange-red sky, the sisters and the aunties and the dadis and the phabis all swooped down to the entrance of our house on their huge, silver-tipped wings, bearing presents for me in their talon-tipped hands.

And such presents! Chachee Asha had captured and gift-wrapped a mischievous Caribbean wind; it buffeted the sides of its wicker box in annoyance and puffed bad-temperedly with its efforts. I vaguely recall how hot and spicy its breath was. Little Manju masi, small of wingspan but large of heart, had collected in a jade and brass urn the tears of the crying blue mountain. In my country, at the apex of the mountain range that runs across the central valley joining east to west coast, there sits a blue mountain who is in love with a cloud. She is a monsoon cloud and only passes over the mountain range twice a year. On the first journey she is black, full, and heavy with rain; on the return journey she is light, emptied and smiling. But she never sees the blue mountain below her, and she never will. My old and many-wrinkled Dadima brought the most dramatic gift of all, the nose, lips and earlobes of a lying man. 'There he was,' she told us, 'standing in the market-place selling mangoes whose worms had worms, and asking so much, too. So of course . . .' She made a slicing gesture with the tip of one graceful wing. 'It was a very clean stroke; he hardly made a sound.' My mother strung the nose, lips and earlobes on to a thin ring of silver, and I wore it on the third notch of my leather travelling belt.

So, whilst our sisters made themselves comfortable, fluttering and folding up their wings against the restless breezes that occur at such high altitudes, my mother handed round slices of mango and iced tea, giving gracious thanks to our guests for blessing us with their presence, and my name was decided upon in the customary way. A *thali* of clear water is set in the centre of the circle of women who, at a given sign, all draw up their wings in one smooth gesture until all light is blotted out and only the *thali* and their own thoughts remain within the circle. Upon lowering their wings a name, shining like oil on water, appears on the surface of the *thali*. Once I had been named, my mother from that day on would massage my feet, my hands, and the rapidly swelling stumps between my shoulder blades with hot mustard oil until, after some uncomfortable months during which I scratched and sweated and chafed beneath the pain of the new growth, my wings sprouted like a celebratory handclap and it was time for me to travel.

The morning upon which my travels began was, as I remember it, a most auspicious and crystal-sharp morning. I stood upon the threshold of our home and looked across the ravine to see the whole of our land spread out before me, as tiny and as perfect as an ink-drawn map. The fields, the trees and lakes, symmetrical and many-textured, forming the carpet of the valley floor, enclosed by the rolling curves and hollows of the hills which, coming nearer to us, became snow-capped mountain tops which were our doorsteps and the stairs I would climb down into the land of the wingless souls to begin my adventures. My mother came out to join me. Her eyes were dark pools of sorrow for she knew much time would pass before my return, but like all mothers she understood the only way to truly nurture the strengths and talents of a daughter is to set her free. She placed her hand upon my shoulder, talons catching the new-day sunlight, and slowly folded her wings, a feathered flag of silver and grey rippling like a banner behind her.

'My daughter,' she began, 'you have all that you need.'

By then I was attired in my travelling clothes; sturdy, thick-soled boots would protect my feet from the potholes and sharp stones of the dusty roads that I would have to trudge along, knowing that I could fly the length of them in a minute. Knowing also that the weather conditions at lower altitudes would require some period of adjustment, my mother improvised a garment from a length of cotton cloth, winding it around my body and between my legs so that it offered both protection and freedom of movement. Amongst the tangles and curls of my thick black hair, which in those days hung in unruly snakes to the base of my spine, I fastened feathers from the wings of each of my sisters. When the wind passed over me each feather would whisper in protest, a thousand familiar voices singing out from the nest of my hair. And of course I wore, strapped tightly around my waist, my travelling belt, from which hung cooking pots, utensils, a double-edged dagger, herbs that would heal and poison, and the nose, lips and earlobes of a lying man.

My mother continued. 'You will see much in the land of the wingless that will amaze you. Your eyes will dilate to absorb these wonders, just as the *thali* drew in and absorbed from women's thoughts your maternal name. But you will also witness much that will sorrow you, your child-heart will be sliced into slivers like an overripe fruit, and your tears will rival the tears of the blue mountain. But these tears, like the miracles you observe, must be absorbed silently. Remember, you go as a traveller, not as a leader.'

I opened my mouth to protest but her eyes stopped the words as they sat on my lips.

'These women that you will meet gave up their wings a long time ago; many would laugh at you if you attempted to tell them of their forgotten heritage, and their keepers would try to kill you if they found out what you are, for they are a breed who tend to destroy what they cannot control.'

My heart already felt heavy with helplessness. Seeing my sadness, my mother gently stroked my folded wings, carefully hidden beneath the tightly wound material, and leaned a little closer to my ear.

'However,' she whispered, 'there will be some women, some, whose ears will strain to hear the music of your songs, whose eyes will detect beneath your disguise the shadow of a wing, and the rare few who will feel between their shoulder blades the pricking of feathers where flesh now resides, as if recalling some half-remembered dream from many lives ago. To these women you may be able to communicate a little of what our land and life is about. But be careful, child. Your vision is as yet fresh and unsullied, whilst they bear the weight of many centuries of conditioning, a burden much more heavy than a pair of baby wings.'

And with that, she pushed away a tendril of hair to kiss me on my wide, brown forehead and gave me a push which launched me, open-mouthed and exhilarated, into the pure blue air, wings tilted to harness and ride the powerful currents sucking me down, down, and away.

Travelling alone in the land of the wingless proved a much more complex task than I had imagined. Frankly, I did not realise that my appearance would provoke so much alarm and contempt; as far as I was concerned, my outfit entirely suited the rigours and demands of a mobile lifestyle. However, after enduring the insults and taunts thrown at me because of my walking boots (too masculine), my wraparound dress (too vulgar), and my hairstyle (too provocative), I gradually modified my looks in order to travel more freely amongst these people. I gave up my boots for ordinary open-toed sandals, although it took many moons of painful blisters before my feet adjusted to the flimsiness of the support they offered against the hard, dusty roads. I stopped wearing my robe like a harness strung between my legs and instead hung the material in folds from my travelling belt so that my legs were entirely covered and therefore somewhat restricted if I ever needed to run or climb to a destination.

I also managed to coax my hair into some kind of order by tying up my curls into a loose bun with a length of scented creeper, and displayed all the feathers from my sisters' wings in bunches, swinging from the notches of my leather travelling belt. By modifying my appearance in this manner I was able to move fairly easily from one village to another, but still encountered attitudes that defied any kind of reason. When the land-bound dwellers saw that I was a woman alone, not under the protection of a keeper or guardian, they would regard me with suspicion.

'Has she no husband or father to defend her *izzat*,' the women would whisper to each other, standing in huddles around the village well.

'She emits the stink of shame,' the men would growl, squatting over their tiffin boxes in the midday heat. 'How she stares without modesty. Hussy!' But later on, whilst their women sat indoors in drowsy clusters, a child at each breast, the men would come silently one by one to my sleeping place under some tall tree and offer me a few coins for my body.

When I sang the songs taught to me by my sisters, rousing folk songs which beat out the joys of the freedom of flight, of unimpeded motion through the skies of a woman's desires, or *ghazals* of melancholy, longing laments for the ones whose wings had been clipped by the blind slavekeepers many centuries ago, they did not understand that I sang only for them. My gifts were judged poisonous, subversive, unwomanly.

'Go to the *hijiras*, half-man devil!' They would throw stones and shout in their deep, gruff voices. 'Half demon! Leave our women in peace!' As I left, I would see the women's faces peeping at me from the shelter of their doorways. In most cases the eyes were soulless, lost, not hostile but bewildered. In one or two instances I would glimpse something approaching admiration and suddenly feel a surge of hope. Perhaps, years hence, one of these women would be

100

crouching down kneading dough for the evening meal and a snatch of some tune I had sung, some word I had spoken, would come to her like a benediction, and she would cease her labour and be overcome by a sensation that would be very new and very old all at once, the pricking of sprouting feathers between her shoulder blades, and then she would remember the crazy woman who had visited her village long ago, and understand.

I moved on from village to village, through towns to cities, wide-eyed and absorbing all like the still surface of the water in the *thali*. By the time I had worn out six pairs of sandals I had crossed the ocean surrounding my island home, exchanging temperate winds and balmy skies for the sharp angles and muted shades of far-off, built-up foreign cities. My experiences in these cities were the hardest. There, on the streets bounded by concrete and glass, I saw many men and women seemingly working together, side by side, with no divisions. I looked hard into the eyes of these tall, high-stepping women with confident chins and hands full of papers who moved so swiftly – surely they were trying to fly!

But alas, on closer inspection I saw that their shoulders were not arched to support the span of two wings but hunched to bear up the weight of their guilt. For each time they tensed up their muscles, preparing to leap into the wide skies of their desires, some wingless man, a father, a brother, most often a lover, would bleat out for the comfort of a female hand, would point accusing fingers at neglected children, would issue warnings about the gossip going on behind closed doors. And then the woman would be torn in two, her heart somewhere in the clouds and her feet nailed down to the concrete floor. These women, I felt, had the hardest struggle of all. Yet there were many who listened to my songs, and in some I saw the light of understanding begin to glimmer in their eyes and they would look to their daughters sitting at their feet and smile a secret smile, making plans for a future flying career. That was a most cherished sign of hope.

It was an unwritten rule that I would not visit any place more than once; in some cases it would have been dangerous to do so but on a practical level I had so much to see and so little time in which to see it. However, there are exceptions to every rule, although

101

upon entering the grey sprawling mass of town in that particular rainy land, I never thought I should have occasion to visit it again. This particular town was depressingly similar to many of the others I had already visited in that vicinity, rows of small, squat-faced houses, many of them run-down and shabby, sharing a bleak uniformity only broken by lone, wistful splashes of colour here and there, a red door, a lurid ornament in a front garden.

It was a house with a few shrivelled flowers growing outside its door that I approached to ask for a drink of water, having travelled six hours without stopping. The woman who came to answer my knocking stopped short in alarm, seeing me. News of my arrival had obviously reached her door before I had. Upon hearing my request she pointed dismissively towards an old stone drinking fountain at the corner of the street. After I had explained that I never drew water from such sources as accusations of me poisoning the water supply inevitably followed, she called exasperatedly into the house and a young girl, presumably her daughter, emerged. She stood at least head and shoulders above her mother, broad-shouldered, muscular, with a long lean torso and square feet planted firmly on the step where she stood staring directly into my face. Silently she accompanied me to the drinking fountain, collected water in a metal bowl which she held out to me, cupping it in one broad-fingered hand. At that point I looked into her eyes and caught my breath. For the first time during my long years of travelling I saw, shining in the large black pupils, the will to fly and the knowledge to do it. With a swift gesture she placed one hand on my back and felt the shape of my neatly folded wings hidden beneath my robe, traced the curve from shoulder muscle to wing tip, letting her fingers ride the bumps of the tightly packed feathers, and said, 'Please sing me a song.'

I remained in that dismal town for a month, meeting the girl secretly in a scrawny patch of woodland behind her house. I sang to her every song I had ever been taught or even vaguely remembered, as often she would spontaneously compose lyrics and tunes of her own imagination. I told her every detail I could recall about my home land, explained to her how, there, she and I would be revered, considered innovative, powerful. She did not seem

102

surprised. She had felt the longing to explore, grow, fly, for many years but had learned through bitter experience to keep them silent, explaining how her mother had been frightened by her talk of travel, how her father and brothers would punish her if these ideas were to become public. I massaged her shoulder blades daily with hot mustard oil and reassured her that she was one of many I had encountered over the years fighting internal battles with her desires, that her desires were not madness, it was only because she was alone and unsupported in her needs that the label of insanity was fixed upon her, and that some day the wingless ones would be in the minority and the world would understand how good and logical and natural it was for young women to fly.

At the end of the month she seemed to have grown twelve inches at least. 'My father is complaining he'll have to marry me off to a Bhatan,' she giggled. We both knew she was joking, of course, she had seen and heard too much about the clouds and stars and wide-open spaces of sky to ever submit to such an earthbound idea. I explained to her that it was time for me to move on. 'Who knows? There may be another sister in the next town just waiting for me to arrive.' Before I left, she sat me down and shyly began unwinding her shawl, all the while smiling, smiling, smiling. There, in the centre of her jutting shoulder blades were two perfect brown stumps. I placed my hand upon them; they were warm and pulsing with new growth.

'You will come back one day?' she asked.

'If you are still here.' I kissed her on her forehead and departed.

It was to be seventy moons later that I would meet her again. During that time I did meet more young women who listened to my songs but not one of them possessed her intuition and clarity of vision. I thought of her often and felt a thrill of anticipation walking through the same stark streets on my way to the house with the faded flowers at the door. But as I approached the house I realised that something was wrong. The house was evidently empty; the old, cracked wood barricading the door indicated it had been abandoned some time ago. I approached a young girl who was standing by the water fountain. By now I was older and perhaps my wrinkles and few grey hairs presented a less threatening front to many. I asked her what had become of the girl and her family.

She shifted uncomfortably before answering, 'They left here long ago. The daughter,' she lowered her voice, 'she brought shame on them.'

'Where is she now?' I persisted.

The girl's eyes dilated with fear. 'They say she has turned into some kind of monster and lives in the woods. She catches babies and eats them. That's what they say.' And with that, she turned abruptly and left.

When I reached the woods it was almost dusk, a warm, close evening with a bone-white moon just beginning to rise. I sat in our usual clearing and waited, listening to the few feeble crickets chirping and the rustle of the leaves on the brittle-thin trees. I did not have to wait long. There was a deep loud cry, so full of longing and loss that circles of pain reverberated through the heavy-hanging air like ripples extending from a pebble dropped into water, and she swooped into the clearing on huge black wings with talons of steel, ten points of light glinting in the shadows. Her hair was matted and hung in wild tangles, her skin was roughened and weather-worn from years of flying against the wind, and her eyes burned with the fire of unfulfilment.

'You said you would come back,' she breathed. 'But after so long . . .'

'I had others to see. You were not the only one.'

'I was the only one who knew. The only one who truly understood your songs and remembered them word for word, note for note.'

As if to prove her point, she sang a snatch from a free-flight *ghazal*, her pure voice bouncing off the tree trunks, throwing back a multi-layered echo which vibrated with energy.

'I sing my own songs now,' she told me.

'In here?' I asked her. 'Who hears them here except for the crickets and the wind?'

'Where else was there?' she cried out in anguish. 'Where else could I go? You massaged my wings into being but you left me no map to your land. You filled my head with dreams of soaring free but you left me living here amongst the wingless ones.'

104

She came closer, so close that I could smell the bitterness on her breath.

'Do you know, two months after you left, my parents married me off to a sixty-year-old tailor. I stayed with him but I never stopped singing your songs to myself whilst I cooked and cleaned and bore two children until, one day, I suddenly realised I could not remember one single tune, and my shoulders became hunched to carry the weight of my duties instead of being arched to support the span of my wings. So I left and came here to wait for you. And as I waited, I remembered all the lessons you had taught me, lessons of patience and trust and fortitude and faith that, one day, the wingless ones would be in the minority. And then I understood how futile it is to wait – for anything.'

I opened my mouth to protest but she stopped the words as they sat on my lips. She drew herself up to her full height; she had grown, she must have been seven feet tall.

'You go,' she said. 'Go and sing your songs and wait for the miracle to happen. I fly by night to other towns and sometimes even the cities and I sing my own songs and over the time we have been apart I have met and trained one hundred others like me. We do not wait. They in turn have been travelling ever further afield to sing their songs to others. In the daytime our wings are folded and hidden, we do not take foolish risks, but at night, when the wingless ones sleep, we are flying.'

In one single fluid leap she was up and gone; the last I saw of her were the black sails of her glorious wings as she crossed the impassive face of the moon.

Meera Syal

Bird

Like a caged bird
Fluttering her wings,
She cried again
For the cage.
Unable to face that
She was alone
And Free.
The cage door was open.

Shazia Sahail

The Sea and the Sky

Whenever I see
The sea and the sky
Meeting . . .
Whenever I see
The horizon
Blurring . . .
I, frightened
Think of
You and I
Loving . . .
Why does this
Strange fear
Appear . . .
Whenever I see
The sea and the sky
Meeting? . . .
Perhaps the distance
Apart
From where I stand
To you . . .
Is the fear
I feel
Whenever I see
The sea and the sky
Meeting . . .

Shazia Sahail

A Day for Nuggo

Sughra Begum sat on the plush dew-drenched lawn of the *sircari* bungalow, peeling oranges for her daughter's breakfast. It was a cool and crisp December morning in Lahore. 'Eight-thirty and still no power in the sun,' she thought, pulling her shawl closer to her body as a feeble ray of sun caught a glint on her spectacles. Her eyes wandered across the boundary wall to the mud tenements a couple of hundred yards away, taking in the usual untidy details.

'Nuggo's done well this morning,' she remarked in surprised tones to her daughter Raabia, who was munching the oranges moodily, one eye on the newspaper she was half reading.

'Just look at her washing sparkling on the line. She's a good worker really.' Her grey head nodded admiringly. 'Those sheets are white as milk, aren't they?'

'Umm . . .' Raabia affirmed, still more interested in the newspaper than in the conversation.

Moments later she scrambled clumsily to her feet. 'Getting late for college, I better rush.' She gathered her books and attendance register. 'I'll be late for lunch, Ma, there's a staff meeting today.'

Sughra Begum also rose slowly to supervise her housework. She usually started her day with a trip to the kitchen to see what was going on. Sarwari's ten year old hurtled into her large frame with the force of a miniature cannon as she came in bursting with the excitement of her news. 'Bibiji, Bibiji,' she panted, 'Nuggo Baji's had a baby boy!'

'Calm down, slowly now,' Sarwari admonished gently as she stirred the onions roasting on the fire.

'Thank God, thank God,' Sughra Begum's hands rose automatically in a gesture of prayer and almost immediately she hurried out her next question as her kind heart responded to the announcement with a rapid association of remembered pain surrounding a similar event thirty odd years ago.

'How is she? How is Nuggo?'

'She's well, Begum Sahib, she's fine,' beamed Sarwari. 'But I can tell you, it was a tough birth, Bibiji. Samuel got the midwife at about ten o'clock but she had to stay for most of the night. She said the baby's head wasn't in the right place. The pains came strong but it wouldn't turn. I think it was a miracle that they found a black cockerel for the sacrifice at that time of night. The moment the blade touched the bird's jugular the baby moved. It came out feet first . . . What are you doing listening to grown-ups?' Off you go to school, she interjected suddenly, noticing her daughter's deep interest in the conversation.

'Anyway, Bibiji, they say babies who are born the wrong way round are very lucky. Tell you the truth I think Nuggo's very lucky, too; it's always dicey when it's like that. And she's some girl. Two hours after the baby came she was up washing clothes.'

Sughra Begum's jaw dropped in astonishment. She sat down, forefinger on cheek, nodding her head in strong disapproval of such conduct. 'Her bones,' she thought admiringly, 'must consist of some superhuman element.'

She ordered an extra half litre of milk for Nuggo. 'Boil it and take it round,' she instructed Sarwari. 'She must have at least two glasses of milk a day.'

Sarwari enthusiastically followed her instructions, glad to be part of this act of kindness which gave her another chance to visit the new arrival. She was full of chatter when she came to see Nuggo though she took every care not to allow the saucepan to touch Nuggo's clay jug. Nuggo didn't seem to notice this.

She was quite grateful for the little gesture. She liked hot milk. She'd been too excited to sleep all night. It was her first son. She kept turning her head to look at him in astonished delight. His tiny fingers were curled into tight fists as he swung in a makeshift improvised hammock, blissfully asleep.

Her back ached and she still felt shivery after the traumatic birth and her midnight session of washing. On and off her husband had kept on calling to her to leave the washing alone. As he dozed, proud father of a son after the excitement and anxiety of the early part of the night, he felt guiltily aware that she oughtn't to be in the cold washing clothes so soon after childbirth. He remembered his own mother had cared for all his sisters at similar times. They were always pampered for the first few weeks but poor Nuggo's mother was dead and his own mother had moved to Dubai to live with her oldest son.

Nuggo, strong and independent at all times, refused to go to bed without getting rid of what she described as the 'muck and yuck' of childbirth. People would be dropping by to see the baby tomorrow, she'd argued, and in their one-roomed house where could she hide piles of dirty washing? He knew she was right. And who else would wash the sheets if she didn't? she'd asked.

'Yes, that's true, too,' he thought. 'Who else?' And so, he slept.

After the euphoric first week life settled down into its old drab routine. Two weeks later Nuggo had returned to her job at the bungalow, dusting, sweeping and washing clothes in lieu of a small salary, her lunch and the privilege of occupying their shabby home. She found it a little tiring to fit in the work of three bungalows now that she had a tyrannical slave driver in residence. Every two hours he screamed for attention and wherever she was she had to down tools and return to attend to him. If she was out of earshot her own body would give her the signal, her breasts tightening and tingling with the increased flow of milk which brimmed over if she was late.

Gradually the strain began to tell. Her lively brisk movements slowed down a little, her dark brown skin which had always glowed with good health paled and dulled a little, and her careful tidiness slackened to a slightly unkempt look. At the bungalow everyone was getting fed up with her trips home. If it hadn't been for the fact that she washed and ironed beautifully, that only Nuggo could remember which shirts belonged to whom and have everyone's clothes and shoes laid out ready for the morning just the way they liked them, Nuggo would have got the sack ages ago. As it was, everyone had become so dependent on her that they continued to put up with her 'time out', putting it down to their own charitable thoughtfulness for the baby and her.

The baby thrived in spite of the makeshift arrangements for his care and frequent tumbles out of the hammock on to the soft muddy floor of his humble abode. Nuggo painted a large black spot on his forehead with kohl each morning to protect him from the evil eye.

As soon as he was old enough to toddle after her, piece of dry chappati clutched between his fingers, Nuggo announced to Sughra Begum that she was pregnant again. Even that placid lady was a little irritated with this state of affairs and all that it spelt for the future . . . a tired Nuggo made inefficient by a trail of toddlers behind her, cluttering their home and keeping them waiting for every little chore. But she said nothing; that was left to Raabia, who bombarded Nuggo with a lecture on the value of birth control and the hazards of overpopulating the world.

Nuggo remained silent, more aware herself this time of the burdensome implications of another baby's arrival and the greater need for money which constant inflation and a larger family demanded. She had struggled to keep her two other afternoon jobs but had found it impossible.

The following year Nuggo had another baby boy. Her husband had moved on from being a sweeper with the Municipal Board to being a night watchman at Holy Family Hospital, and this had the advantage of bringing them not only more money but also a forced abstention from their sex life, which Nuggo felt might help in delaying a third pregnancy. By the time Samuel returned from work the little community was already astir and no one in their right minds would attempt an amorous interlude by daylight in the limited privacy of those dwellings. In fact they got very little opportunity to even talk to each other.

One morning, as Samuel was trying to sleep in the clamour of daylight which surrounded him, he casually mentioned to Nuggo that there were now so few sweepers that the municipality jobs were going a-begging, and they were even taking on women, he'd heard. Nuggo, ever short of money, mulled over this piece of information for the whole day and then decided that she must try to enlist herself for road sweeping. She knew she'd get three times the money for much less work. Samuel demurred and raised several objections but Nuggo countered them all. And then began to plan her strategy on how to obtain Sughra Begum's consent.

The following week she started her new job. They all reported at the Central Depot at five in the morning and then truckloads would be sent out to various sites. By nine they would be on their way back to the depot. Nuggo had only signed on for a four-hour shift. Samuel, who returned home about seven, would babysit in a rough and ready fashion till she returned.

Sughra Begum was not too pleased with the adjustment she'd been asked to make in the timings for Nuggo's work in her house, but she had little choice. She was well aware that there was now a real and serious shortage of sweepers in the city and then they were all so used to Nuggo.

Nuggo did not mind her new job and she really liked the money she was getting. The work was physically more strenuous but the hours were immutably fixed and the wages were never late. She enjoyed the change of surroundings and finding new friends amongst the droves of women who arrived every morning from Raajgadh.

Nuggo still remembered Raajgadh from trips she used to make with her mother to see an aunt who lived there. Every year the rains would flood them out, wrecking their flimsy shelters and claiming two or three lives. When the gullies retracted to their old watermarks, everyone returned to their crumbling and rotting *jhuggies* to salvage the remains, helping each other cheerfully. The smell, the dirt and the flies which encrusted the shanty town were submerged under the warmth, friendship and security that was generated during times of stress. Everyone knew everyone. The children were allowed to play and run around as far as its borders without fear. Sometimes the police raided. Word would get round, 'the *tullas* are coming!' An elaborate act of 'moving out' was performed for their benefit as they stood with vicious-looking batons swinging from their wrists. As soon as the *tullas* left, the Raajgadhians would unpack and spread themselves out again.

Of all her friends from Raajgadh, Nuggo's favourite was Raagni.

Though she felt the greatest admiration for her, at times, she also felt sorry for her. Raagni had no children and a husband who was 'bad' with other women. Nuggo could understand her refusal to live with him, though Raagni's own family were furious with her decision to separate. She kept herself busy and happy by taking on all sorts of activities ranging from matchmaking and fund-raising to sitting on committees and organising petitions. Since volunteers like Raagni were a rare breed, she soon found that she had acquired tremendous influence amongst the local groups. Her education had been minimal but she had a phenomenal memory and a boundless interest in everything. She had vast reserves of information about matters which no one else around her knew anything about, and this made her a great figure of fascination for everyone. Nuggo loved her company, thirsting forever for more of her conversation, which ranged in a single breath from politics to pickled chillies. But they never had much time together.

'Come on Friday,' Raagni would say, but though on Fridays there was no road sweeping Nuggo still worked for Sughra Begum and had enough to do in her own home.

'But that's all wrong,' said Raagni. 'Surely you must have a day off in the week.'

Nuggo said nothing. It was a thought which hadn't occurred to her, but Raagni did not forget this issue. It troubled her deeply that large numbers of their community were probably working seven days a week, like Nuggo. She set about thinking and planning, talking to the other committee wallahs and their local trade union, and then came up with the answer. They would all have to ask their own employers. Each individual member of their community who was in domestic service had to ask for a day off in the week. There was no other way. Most of the sweepers in the city were Christians, and the union wallahs all felt that their day off should be Sunday, not Friday, since they were all church-goers. This meant that all those sweepers who were municipal workers had to campaign for a change in the rules which would allow them to observe Sunday as their holiday. It seemed to be a bigger problem than the first one.

But Raagni was undeterred. She had access to a highly elaborate

113

network of communications which had grown in the sweeper community entirely through the activities of the busy-bee Raajgadhians. This network buzzed with messages for a few days. The trade union, which consisted mainly of the municipal workers, decided that they should all campaign for fewer working hours and for a day off on Sundays for all their working members, irrespective of who they were working for. The demand was put forward and, as expected, was refused.

Nuggo laughed when she heard all this.

'You're a simpleton! D'you think it's possible for us poor people to change things? The world's not going to change that easily and that only so I can visit you on Sunday. It's impossible.'

Raagni was unmoved. 'You'll see,' she said with her chin firmly set. 'Besides, it's not just for you. It's for *all* of us. And we do count. If we stick together we'll be strong. We owe it to each other.' Then she remembered and swung round on her. 'And you, what have you done so far? Have you spoken to your Sughra Begum, or not?'

Nuggo had to confess sheepishly that she had not got round to it yet. In fact, inwardly, she was still not sure if she would really be able to ask for herself. But she had underestimated the strength of feeling in the community about the issue, and the effectiveness of the relatively young trade union.

The following week the union proposed strike action to its members and got their approval. In less than a week the citizens of Lahore began to feel the pinch. The city's sanitation depended heavily on a labour-intensive scheme of organisation. The heat of summer and the flies buzzing around the mounds of filth rising to new peaks each day constituted a health hazard which could not be ignored.

Just as the workers were reaching the point where they couldn't afford to remain away from work any more, the Municipal Board of Lahore caved in and to their sheer, unbelieving delight they found that they had won most of their demands. Chief amongst them was the demand for a holiday on Sunday for all practising Christians who wished to claim Sunday as their day of rest.

There was great jubilation in Raajgadh that night as sweetmeats were passed round and people blew their last few *paisas* on

114

fireworks, secure in the knowledge that they'd be returning to work the next day in triumph, proclaiming even more power to the workers.

But as the excitement and celebrations died down over the following weeks it became apparent that some of the privately employed sweepers were not really benefiting from the new rule. Raagni, who was a tireless campaigner, was determined to ensure that everyone should get a justly deserved day of rest in the week. She would go to visit and support workers who were having difficulty obtaining time off, sometimes because they were too afraid to ask and sometimes because they'd asked and been refused. Soon it became apparent that, at least, from Raajgadh, which was the stronghold of the sweeping community, no one left for work on a Sunday morning and if there were any chinks in the unity of Christian workers they were mostly being caused by people who lived in isolation in servants' quarters or in much smaller settlements than Raajgadh.

Predictably, one such offender was Nuggo. All her work-long life Samuel's mother had worked in the white bungalow and Samuel, like his poor mother, was completely in awe of Sughra Begum. He strictly forbade Nuggo to speak to the Begum Sahib about a day off. She'd always been kind to them, advancing wages ahead of time and letting them build those unsightly homesteads alongside the boundary wall. They owed her some loyalty for that. How could they offend her?

Every morning Raagni would inquisition her, 'Did you ask your Begum Sahib?' and follow her confession with a lecture on her debt to the community and then threaten to come and see Sughra Begum herself.

'Oh, please don't. That really isn't needed,' Nuggo would plead, trying to conceal her panic at the suggestion.

Almost three weeks passed by with Nuggo presenting Samuel's arguments to Raagni and hers to him each day, hoping to convince one of them so that somehow the issue would die or go away, but neither would be persuaded. She was utterly frustrated with being at the heart of a controversy which seemed insoluble. She hadn't really considered herself at all, but the arguments on either side

115

seemed both convincing and sound to her. She didn't know what to do.

The unasked question simmered within her all the time with a more personal immediacy than Samuel or Raagni could have imagined. It would pop up before her tantalizingly as she dragged the large merciless bundle of washing out of the linen bin and again rise before her as she bent her aching back to sweep up the rubbish in the backyard and yet again burst upon her consciousness as she faced the bottomless pit of the ironing basket.

Sughra Begum and her family were aware of the 'Sunday, Day Off' campaign and of the results it had produced, but said nothing. They knew that if Nuggo made the demand they might have to concede it but they were not going to make it easy for her.

Nuggo, tired of work, tired of the arguments wrenching her in opposite directions, trudged slowly to work on the fourth Sunday after most of her other fellow workers had given up doing so. She felt both dejected and guilty.

Raabia was rushing around trying to leave for college. 'Ah,' she said as soon as she saw Nuggo, 'I'm so glad you've turned up at last, Nuggo, I'm really getting late. Hurry up and iron this dupatta quickly before you do anything else.'

Nuggo went obediently to get the ironing board out of the cupboard, forgetting her grouse for a couple of minutes in her effort to hurry. She was only halfway through when her older son, who was barely three, appeared in the doorway.

'The baby's crying, Ma,' he piped in his childish level tones.

'Why? He was fine when I left, sound asleep.' Nuggo felt a little irritated.

Raabia shooed him off in her customary style. 'Okay, okay. She's coming in a minute. Go and find your father for a change and leave her alone. The minute she comes in they start sending messages . . .' she carried on grumbling.

But Qasim just stood there looking at his mother. 'He's really crying, Ma,' he repeated.

'I said she's coming. Off you go now,' Raabia interrupted more sharply than usual, before Nuggo could formulate a reply.

The peremptory note in her voice caused something to snap

within Nuggo's heart. Perhaps the last lingering threads of doubt and courtesy which had held her back. She suddenly knew what she had to do and why.

She looked at Raabia squarely in the eyes as she handed her the dupatta she was ironing and said in measured tones, 'I'm going now, Raabia Bibi. I won't be working on Sundays any more. I'll be back tomorrow if Begum Sahib still wants me to work here.'

'What utter brazen cheek!' Raabia hissed to her mother in a flustered rage. 'I told you they do not deserve all your kindness and generosity, the miserable whining ingrates. "Won't be working on Sundays any more . . ." What unspeakable nerve after all you've done for them. Serves you right anyway. She wouldn't have had the guts if you'd been a bit more firm from the start.'

Sughra Begum, who felt more than a little betrayed by Nuggo's sudden assertion of her rights, sat shaking her head in solemn bewilderment, certain that Samuel's mother would not have been so ungrateful and rebellious. What was the world coming to? No loyalty, no respect for your elders and betters. Raabia was right, she decided, it wasn't worth being kind to these people. She came to the decision that she ought to be firmer and decided to threaten Nuggo with eviction if she didn't withdraw her ultimatum. She felt calmer after that and in control of the situation.

No sooner had Nuggo settled her crying baby than that decision followed her: she either had to return to work or vacate the premises within a day. The five families which clustered scruffily together around the compound were in fact quite divided. The electrician and his family always saw themselves as different and a cut above the rest and were not really interested in the affair. The gatekeeper, who was a Pathan, disliked Samuel and Nuggo for being so popular with Begum Sahib and so was secretly a little pleased to see them in disfavour for a change. Only the Dhobi and his family cared enough to offer to leave in protest if Nuggo was forced out of her home, but her friend Sarwari was too poor to be able to offer that kind of support. She was neither in a position to negotiate terms for herself, nor able to comprehend how a worker could ever hope to do so. She just delivered Sughra Begum's message sadly and pleaded with Nuggo to return and ask to be forgiven.

'Apologise. Go and apologise, Nuggo. For goodness' sake, go.'
All day Samuel begged her but Nuggo just sat there, refusing to do
so. She felt deeply hurt and humiliated. The angry taste of tears of
resentment kept choking her and a sudden sense of being exposed
shamed her senses. She did not know what they would or could do
next. Somehow this was an exigency which had not presented itself
to her.

'I haven't done anything wrong,' she said to Samuel over and
over again, but he seemed not to hear this.

Raagni had intended her visit as a pleasant surprise but when she
walked in she sensed an atmosphere. They both rose at once in
embarrassment.

'All because of this stupid bitch!' thought Samuel, looking at her
resentfully and noticing that she was younger than he'd reckoned
and much darker than Nuggo.

'And so what's the problem then?' she asked calmly when she'd
heard the story without surprise.

'What do we do now?' asked Nuggo, 'Where do we go?'

'To Raajgadh, of course. You weren't going to return to work
for these selfish, unjust people, were you?' She seemed genuinely
surprised.

'Of course she was,' Samuel interrupted rather rudely. 'We
can't live in Raajgadh juggling between life and death every
monsoon. It stinks. It is for the poorest of the poor. We don't want
to go there. Nuggo will apologise tonight and Begum Sahib will
surely forgive her. I know she is kind.'

Nuggo repeated almost mechanically, 'I have not done anything
wrong.' Samuel took no notice of her but she got up with a
purposeful air to pack her few worldly goods into large shapeless
bundles knotted up in old bedsheets.

'Poorest of the poor we might be but we are happier and more
independent than most others,' Raagni taunted acidly.

Samuel said nothing, only stared at her with hatred for causing
all this disruption. 'Evil black bitch!' he thought spitefully. 'No
wonder her husband didn't want her.' But his eyes lingered on her
ample bosom just a fraction longer than he'd intended. She carried
herself with the ease of a man of the world. He envied her

118

assuredness and swagger.

Doggedly Nuggo continued to pack through the afternoon, attending to the children in between as they screamed, unsettled by the chaos which had been unleashed around them. Amidst the confusion arrived a message of reconciliation from Sughra Begum. She'd decided to reconsider Nuggo's request for the day off.

Raagni had already left to make arrangements for them to live in Raajgadh. Samuel was getting ready to leave for work, quite nonplussed by his wife's uncharacteristic intransigence. He cursed Raagni yet again . . . devil woman with an ash-blackened womb . . .

Sughra Begum's message lifted his spirits. It was a twist in the circumstances which suited him, the perfect solution to the deadlock. 'Begum Sahib is kind. I knew it. She really is, isn't she?' He addressed the question to no one in particular.

Nuggo said nothing in reply to that. Her eyes met Sarwari's in an attempt to confirm her own rebellious opinion on that subject, finding nothing but bland relief in Sarwari's face. Her tone was laced with defiance as she conceded in a sharp voice, 'All right, then! Tell her I shall return to work tomorrow.'

Rukhsana Ahmad

Games

Games people play are only those that made the playground ring with laughs, cries, shifting allegiances, broken alliances, and fights over territorial rights. Ours was the corner between the wall of the boys' school and the kitchen; any who ventured too near would pay the penalty. Margaret elicited payment in pain, each groan planting a rosy smile on her face, unrelenting till she'd harvested a bouquet of pleasure, made fragrant by the appropriation of any money that might be jingling in the trespasser's pockets.

I, who was five foot nothing, would stay in the shadows, and all who saw me would deride me for not being a thing worth anything, and the only reason they did not catch me in a corner of the cloakroom or alone on a dark winter's night was the power of Margaret's muscles, whose strength they had felt and whose loyalty they knew was the umbrella under which I walked in freedom. I smiled weakly and feigned terror and let them have their laughs and sniggers, for who was to know of the Woman behind the Woman? Who was to know that quiet words whispered into Margaret's ear were the key that made her motors run, the brain that directed the brawn? I would pull my coat close, smile into its collar and show a scared face to any I happened to meet.

Memories of those school years gone by, trailing my feet as I walk through the pouring rain and stop to shelter under a doorway; my eyes go through the glass to the TV screens where a child cries on a hospital bed, and homes lie ruined in heaps of dust, shifting to another set where a shouting crowd hold guns aloft in angry resentment, yet another where contestants sweat anxiety to win and possess inviting prizes, the last, but not least, a teapot scene from the street. My throat itches and, not knowing whether to scratch or laugh, I give up waiting for the rain to stop and step out to carry on home. Only to get drenched by the spray of a passing truck and a leer of lust as his passenger peers out.

The door swings open on the phone's shrill ringing. Margaret calling, telling me she's gathered another scalp for her belt and do I want a share? Her invitation is like a match to a fuse as I change and call a taxi. The locket falls out as I rearrange my bag and picking it up I throw it out the window, as I'd thrown him away, undeterred by his disbelieving eyes. A whitey who claimed to be all Right through and through, got lost in my bed and started talking Liberal Left, and I had no mercy for he had no principles, for if he had he wouldn't have turned himself inside out and shown me that the writing on his guts was always carbon copy only.

Margaret was gleefully putting away her toys. 'Such fun,' she said, 'I've had today. Look at my loot and count it well. Money and a radio and six golden bangles.' Picking them up she jangled them around and told me how they were tinkling and sparkling round the dark wrist of an Asian lady.

'I caught her in a corner. Remember the school corner? I was sweet to her, oh, so gentle. They're gentle people, these Asians are.' Then she looked at me and looked away, not knowing the rights and wrongs of what she had said. I took the bangles and slipped them over my own dark wrist, thinking of the ones that would never be mine, bequeathed to me by parents proud at a wedding lavish with music and song, full of sorrow and love, the bittersweet taste of lives changing.

Lives changed forever at the hands of thugs: shouting 'whites only', citing the Union Jack; playground bullies wanting to show off, scattering on the street the flesh, blood and bones of a man and a woman on their way home through England's evening darkness. Blood stained a pavement, but not for long as the rains came and washed it clean. So well erased, so soon disappearing the memory became suspect as the agent of imagination, as my living and growing in a children's home ruptured the past away from the present.

'Er, these would go well with them,' holding out a head pendant. Another relic of rituals that will never be. I shook my head and she said, 'Well, then, let's go. I've arranged an arrangement,' quickly scurrying to gather her gear. I thought it strange but let it be and didn't know till we pulled up on a car park corner and Reggie rose from reclining on his bike. The sunset behind him cast a rosy aura as he sauntered towards us, hips swaying under a heavy, metal-studded belt. Margaret jumped out and walked around to meet him. Their hands touched in a brief greeting and I thought, 'Good grief, how long's this been going on?' Margaret brought him over and I knew they both expected me to get out and do the polite, pretend nothing had happened behind my back. Oh, no. I stayed put. Let them come to me.

Reggie offered me a packet of cigarettes and I said, 'Haven't you read the government health warning on them?'

'Never was much good at school,' he said. 'But these ain't fags. They're thanks.'

Margaret took me home and opened a bottle and tried to convince me that what she'd done was for the best. Opening the cigarette packet she shook it out on the table, releasing a medallion which rolled over the polished surface in a tinkling circle till it ran out of motion and fell flat into silence.

'I'm going to move,' I said. 'Too many people know where I live. Did love lead you into this lunacy?' Margaret picked up the medallion and dropping it into her wine lifted the glass in a toast. Not waiting for me to join, but eyes wide-looking all the time into mine, she drained it to the bottom.

'Time for pruning,' she said. 'Getting too big for their boots they were, thinking we was scared to right our wrongs. Reggie hit them where it hurt, taken Pandoro out of our way. We've got back the territory that used to be ours and more.'

'We're small-time small fry. Two teeny-weeny bitches too titchy to talk territory.'

Margaret stood up, trailing her fingers along my ceiling. 'I couldn't say no when Reggie needed our help. A team effort with gains that go both ways. We've used him in the past, we'll need to use him again. He's cleared our patch of the weeds that was going to choke us. We can grow now.'

'Danger, we didn't need . . . You can go now,' I said.

She dropped a tear on the table. I gave her a tissue to wipe it off and then another as the monsoons came and I knew there could be no division between us, for we were each other's creation and the acts of one bound the hands of the other. Now we'd have to learn to look over our shoulders, guard each other's backs because Pandoro's medallion had become a magnet of fire and as the acrid smell seeped through our words Margaret poured another glassful and talked of information about their plans and how it was a fight for survival and they who attack first live to attack another day. Someone banging on the door and we both stand up as muffled shouts and more bangs follow; Margaret is picking up Reggie's belt and buckling it tight around her waist and my derision at this love token is silenced on my lips as I notice the smoke crawling snakelike under the door.

The neighbours were helpfully going wild with buckets of water, drenching us through as we rushed out, our feet going yucky in puddles of ashes of what was once an expensive rug. Sympathy and comforting arms and someone's kitchen become a tea canteen as mugs passed round and much talk made of racist hooligans.

'Who do they bleedin' think they are?' asked Mrs Prindle from across the corridor, voice rising in indignation. 'Think they run the bleedin' country, they do. It's us ordinary people what get caught in the middle all the time. Time was when there was some decency and respect for law and order. You knew who . . .'

'Vigilante committee.' The man with the droopy moustache cut in sharp as a knife, flipping open his notebook and snapping on his Biro. My eyes opened wide and I thought I could be impressed. He asked for volunteers, explaining the need for a defensive strategy. Like pulling out a plug, their brave talk trickled out, flushed down by a rush of questions, suggestions, suppositions, modifications and the thin end of the wedge of immovable excuses. Droopy moustache looked at me and said 'Sorry' and offered to help with 'pressuring the police. They don't do much do they?' Margaret caught a coughing fit and I rushed her back to pour honey down her throat and she saw my look was a knife following it down.

Margaret gagged and threw up on the kitchen floor.

Time to split, I thought, say goodbye and turn my back, take my road and walk away. We'd done well; we'd had enough for flesh and spirit: enough for the body's sustenance and enough for the pleasures of the world. Margaret had cracked open the fragile shell of our little lives and exposed us to dangers far beyond the scope of our strength.

I dragged out the old tin trunk and, lifting it on to the bed, pushed back the top. They stared at me. They always stared at me when I was at a beginning and at an end. She sitting on his left, her face draped in a bordered, embroidered dupatta, its graceful folds falling around her face and framing a pair of *jhumka* earrings, his double-breasted suit tightly buttoned and turban tied to a peak: their cheeks glowing pink with the photographer's touch up. My fingers traced the shape of the earrings, my ears tingling to own them. Did they get crushed in the blows and kicks that rained down on her, were they ripped from her ears? Are they now sitting in some white woman's jewellery box? She probably thinks they came in the sale from Woolworth's.

A hand came forward and closed the trunk shut. Margaret was shaking her head. 'They work fast,' she said, 'and they never let go.' The smell of the fire still lingered everywhere and I who had thought that Margaret was my puppet now felt the strings on my head and limbs.

Consultations in a pub, with Reggie who sneered at me, caressed Margaret's hand and ordered yet another pint.

'Here's looking at you, babe.' Eyes on me, hand between Margaret's knees. I suggested conciliation with the others, a return to the time before Pandoro's medallion tinkled its awful circle on my table. They jeered and laughed, and Margaret said, 'This can't be you! You wanting to retreat! Wanting to keep your head down! Wanting a quiet life at any cost!'

'We're out of our depth.' No joke intended, but they opened their mouths and laughed a lot; these two were convinced a winning streak was theirs, that their roller coaster could only take them higher and higher and never dip tumbling into disaster. Mine was the unwanted carping-nagging voice of doom. The laughter gradually faded from their faces and gathered in the air around me as he said, 'You go watch telly or take up aerobics or something; we'll finish the job, mop up the leftovers. The earnings, we'll come back to share with you. Say ta to Maggie.'

We parted company outside the pub. I watched Margaret clinging to him like a legless limpet and refused to step back as Reggie's revs mounted the pavement and zoomed in on a curve towards me. Margaret laughed and thought it a huge joke, her hand chucking back a kiss to me.

I wouldn't go with them, but I would be their menial, the thing to whom they gave subsistence and sustenance, their rent propping up her roof and keeping warm her room, her prison. They provided and thus obviated the need to forage outside, for who knows what unhealthy thoughts can enter the mind of the discontented? Telling tales in the comfort of a fuzz station may become her line of defence, or crossing over to the other side whose strength she reckons of greater power, and at the very least a degree more potent for being fuelled by the code of revenge.

I thought nothing of anything. Amputated of action, my thoughts sought out a perpetual amnesia till the day I entered my flat to find Pandoro materialised: a ghost from the past sitting unsmiling in my chair by the window, medallion glinting on his neck.

'Not his, then whose? The old one that siamesed with Agni*?' think I, mind's net trawling fast for explanation. 'If not him, then who?' At his kind invitation I removed my coat and made myself comfortable, as he reeled off the answers to my unspoken questions.

'This chain is shorter, doesn't give as good a grip for strangling from behind as the last one. You're in bad company. Never known anyone do a sloppy job like this one your friends were doing. The secret of success is to double check. I am supposed to be dead as a dodo doornail. Yes?' I couldn't agree more, but didn't intend to say

*Goddess of fire.

125

so aloud. 'What would you say to a job?' I kept mum and didn't say nothing. 'What would they say, them that's good at bungling, to talks? A kind of mini-summit, shall we say?'

'No.' For they would, and what's the point in chasing a hopeless hope?

'Come,' he said, 'an invitation to stay with us awhile. Enjoy our hospitality. We'll talk, get acquainted. Maybe we'll find some things in common.'

He tinkled his bell and six appeared. Rats into men, I thought, come to guard this Cinderella on his journeys, his buffer against midnight chiming its devastation, reducing Pandoro to the old rat race. Rats again! Two more appeared with a wheelchair. Not for me, but Pandoro. Captured by shock, I lost the one chance to slip out into escape.

With the blindfold off, I saw the room was pretty, all blue and white, adorned and highlighted with touches of gold, pink roses intertwining through the bars around the windows. 'Burglary,' said one of the Rats as he backed out. 'Terrible problem round here,' double locking the door behind him.

Margaret had given herself away through infatuation; I was shut away through circumstances. Either way, neither could now control the happenings to us and around us. Though Pandoro offered me a key as he poured out the wine and recommended the lamb tikka. His pretensions, far outstripping the walls of this semi-detached, aroused no humour in me; I was busy trying hard to turn into granite and blind my eyes to what was to come.

The key he wanted was the calligraphy of my tongue: tell all and rewards would be mine. I, reluctant, tongue-tied by the umbilical cord between Margaret and me. Pandoro's programme of self-gentrification (connoisseur of culture, man of refinement) would never allow him to utilise brutal force against me; instead they led me into a cellar heavy with the darkness that gives birth to hideous fears where myself becomes my own enemy. Days spent hunched in a corner, squeezing into the cracks between walls, turning, shivering away from the monsters crawling out of that frightening precarious childhood. Did Pandoro know it wouldn't be long before I unfurled what I knew, gave them the tacks to trip up

Maggie and Reggie? Smooth the path for them to appropriate that which should never have been theirs? A giveaway, takeaway! Gifted by Maggie's greed and Reggie's vanity.

Proud of myself, I was holding out, congratulating myself on my endurance, till the day Pandoro invited me to afternoon tea and for my entertainment produced the photo of Them from my trunk. I balled my hands, tucked them away under rigid, folded arms, lest they flash out, and snatch.

Bored with our desultory conversation, Pandoro picked up the picture and absent-mindedly toyed with it; hit by an idea he unpinned his tiepin and proceeded to amuse himself by pushing it in and out the photo, working inwards, from the outside, getting nearer to the face, lips and eyes.

'Probably not much use to you,' I said, 'what I've got to tell,' preparing the ground for the grass.

'I'll decide about that,' holding the photo up to the light, the pricked holes glowing stars of bulb light. I talked, told all I knew of Maggie's and Reggie's plans, the extent of their knowledge, their defences and hideouts; my words muffled by the growing heap of ashes in my mouth. 'Not very imaginative,' he said. 'You like these,' pushing forward a plastic box. I couldn't care. I wasn't me. My years with Margaret bartered for a battered photo.

Opening the box, he peeled back the pink paper, ever synonymous with Indian gold, and lifted out my mother's earrings. Not so. Memory can forget or it can replicate in minutest detail and mine knew the difference between a nick and a glint. 'You seem to like such things,' he said going back to deseeding a grape.

'Did!' I said. Betray your past and it'll sour all you ever held dear.

'For the present, you must be my guest a while longer. Afterwards you can go wherever you want.'

'That's foolish of you.'

His eyes were full of an unaccustomed pity, as the day came and the door opened for me to leave. Who was he and how dare he and I shot a look to shear his pity away. Some of the flying flak must have stuck on to me and weighted my feet. I couldn't move, standing at the threshold, looking unseeing at the gate.

'You're no worse off than me,' said Pandoro tapping his legs. He wasn't foolish. Knowing, what was what, was what he was.

No longer puppet-master, no longer a puppet, hands empty, body bare of Margaret's presence, the days spent in a useless search. No one knew, or no one talked. It could be she'd never existed. I bought a belt the likes of the one Reggie gave to Maggie and took to riding motorbikes, and for the first time settled down to scrabble among the rat race, sell my labour and time to an employer. I took up what is known as a steady job and made do on the attached miserly income. I couldn't understand why people accepted, actually hunted and longed for this self-same opportunity to sell self day after day for a few pounds a day. Enough to buy beer and chips, nothing left for the nourishment of those parts of us that delight and deliver the unknown in words known, in pictures, music or movement. Famine stalks the land and no one knows, for all are busy greedily gourmandising on today's cheap offers.

Morality. Some say it is the other name of abstinence; abstinence from what I and Margaret used to do, causing pain to them that lost, accruing pleasure from tricks and cons. No more of that. Girding on fortitude I resolved to be like them, there must be something in it, if so many do it and do it all their lives.

Motorbike messenger woman: carrying parcels, letters, documents and messages. The working hours of night or day took me like a peeping Tom into offices, homes, private and personal lives. Often used as the go-between across no-man's land, the carrier of hostilities from one front to another; try as I might to turn to steel, my flesh felt the bruises of these encounters with the segments of other's lives; pain and passion that cut like jagged glass, growing over the years from little grievances to glowing hate: longings, bitterness, revenge, plots, intrigues. My eyes could find no rest. I had hoped for peace and quiet, hoped to sink into the tranquillity of what I used to call ordinary life. Not so. Bruised by the flying shrapnel of other people's business and emotional warfare, I went back to visit the one who was at least of my kind.

Pandoro was ensconced in a newer, bigger, richer house, more approximate to the pretensions of a suburban yuppie.

We sat over a chintz-covered table and freshly ground, freshly brewed coffee. 'It's the same outside,' my voice said, 'except they mug where the mind hurts; it doesn't leave any bruises, no evidence of anything having been taken, for how do you know it was there in the first place? Love, confidence, truth . . . And they can always say they never did it, never meant to . . .' My voice trailed away, unused to talking at such length.

'I know,' fork gently slicing through a piece of chocolate liqueur gateau.

'I've tried. I can't belong with them.'

'They don't belong with each other. I knew you'd come back.'

'Only for the photo.'

'Not yet.'

He waited, wanted me to say it. Wouldn't offer unless I asked. 'Would you, please, let me join you?' The enemy turned prodigal supplicant returning to the fold. I didn't. Instead asked about Margaret.

Pandoro smiled. 'Doing well for herself, I understand. Last time I heard she was setting up her own business. Terribly sorry, 'fraid I've lost her address.' I could have asked him on my bended knees, for a moment simulating the bend in his. Except it might look like mockery. Except, I doubted it would make any difference.

I stood up, and he smiled his pitying smile again. 'We'll meet again.'

There is no room for manoeuvre, no stepping sideways, tough whichever way you turn. Cosy, it had been with Margaret, us two in our own little world. 'If Reggie hadn't come along' had been a running refrain reeling round my mind. I stopped it. Something else, anything else could have happened, as had happened to them that walked home on a dark night, him in a turban, and her in her dupatta.

'We shall not,' said someone in a book, 'offer hostages to fortune.' I shall not, determined I, keeping time with the pistol-shot revs, hanker any longer over the dead. No more Maggie, no more of them that live in the photo. Speeding away was a shedding of the past; I knew what had gone behind. I didn't know what lay ahead. I would have to learn how to live without them, for I didn't want desperation bringing me back to Pandoro and his smug spider menace. Merging into the traffic was a declaration of intent, to take possession of time and space. She was gone and they were dead, and I would now be my own puppet-master and puppet; this here, one Indian girl no longer running from her inheritance, be it battleground or playground.

Ravinder Randhawa

Veils and Windows

So this is growing up
Being too aware
Too open
Vulnerable to everything.
Feeling unsettled
As veil after veil
Is torn away from
My face.
My mind
My eyes cannot grasp
This world.
Now, there are too many
Windows
To look out of
And into!

So this is being a woman.
Its intensity
Frightens me.
As veil after veil
Of feeling
Gets tangled up.

The flights of fantasy
Dreams, hopes,
Illusions
Shattering.
With the pain
Of reality.
Each month.
An awakening sexuality
What do I do?
Which way to turn?

One more veil
Where do I leave it?
My mind and body
Veiled in torment
Seen through a haze.
Blood red.
So, this is growing up.
I veiled as a woman
Want the peace
Of the very
Young
And of the very
Old.

Shazia Sahail

This poem was written to commemorate the death of Balwant Kaur, an Asian woman who was brutally stabbed to death by her husband in front of her children at the refuge to which she had escaped. The Balwant Kaur campaign held a fund-raising memorial at which this poem was read out.

Blood-Lust to Dust

There you lay oozing
Blood ran cold, Blood ran dry,
A solitary fly buzzing
Stunned by the echo of your death-cries
Stifled by your blood-constricted throat
Brutalised by a knife's gyration

Sister, all your imagined wrongs
That moved his great hairy wrist
Insinuatingly through dark alleyways
Twitching inside an overcoat
Seeking your final submission
Calling out your guts

Children peeking, unbelieving
Your mother and I are talking
Blood-spilling
What kind of talking is that?
Let it be the last

You will not be consigned to dust
Time must not heal
Nor memory conceal
Your blood will not congeal
Our actions

This is not one more obituary,
Not one more nail
Sealing the covers of our oppression
This is but the lifting of the lid
That made us go on seething

Come, we will show men what fear is
When courage stalks a woman's raised fist.

Rahila Gupta

The Will

Usually Archna came down to the kitchen for her breakfast, but this morning she hadn't appeared. Rama, her younger brother's wife, asked the older brother's wife,

'Didi, is Archna all right?'

Didi replied, 'How should I know? I have enough to do without worrying about her.'

Rama decided to go and see for herself. She went up to Archna's room and sat on the edge of the bed. Archna did not move. Rama touched Archna's arm to wake her: its coldness startled her. She ran to the door.

'Didi! Didi! Come quick!'

Didi, who was busy preparing the mid-day meal for the family, turned off the kerosene stove and came out of the kitchen. She went upstairs to the room, where Archna was lying in her bed. She exchanged glances with Rama.

'I don't know who's going to tell Baba.'

Rama thought for a moment of their father-in-law in his room along the corridor. Then Didi spoke again.

'We'll call the doctor, and let him decide what to do.'

They didn't have to wait long. Dr Mitra, who was in his sixties, had been this family's doctor since his youth, and had attended to all the family's births, illnesses and deaths. Dr Mitra began to examine Archna, but looked up almost at once.

'She's dead,' he said. 'Did you know this when you called me?' The two women, who were standing at the foot of the bed, said nothing. The doctor continued his examination.

'Has she been taking her tablets?'

Rama nodded.

'Was she taking them herself?'

'Yes,' said Didi. 'It gave her something to do.'

The doctor looked at her. 'Have her brothers been informed yet?'

'They are on their way home,' Didi replied. 'My father-in-law is next door, if you'd like to talk to him.'

'I'll wait till your husbands arrive.'

The brothers returned home shortly afterwards and received the news of Archna's death. The doctor's diagnosis was that Archna had died in her sleep either because the medicine she'd been taking had weakened her system or because she had taken an overdose. Either way, negligence was a contributory factor.

Archna had known little happiness in the long years of her adult life. At eighteen she had been married off to a man twice her age. Within a year, a daughter had been born, but Archna had never really recovered from her daughter's birth and had slowly succumbed to depression. She and her daughter had come back home to be taken care of by her parents. In the years since then, her sister had been married off in her turn; her brothers had married and brought their wives to the family house; her mother had died; and her father had become an invalid.

The father, Kamalbabu as the neighbours called him – his full name was Kamalkrishna Ray – had been dependent on his sons since his wife's death. He had gathered together some small savings to leave to his children, and was confident that they would look after him in his old age in return. But he had felt less certain about Archna's future. Her death freed him from that anxiety, but he felt an emptiness around him now that she was gone. On her good days, she had always found time to sit by him. His sons and their wives were always busy with their own lives. After Archna's death Kamalbabu's existence narrowed to his small room with its bed and few bits of furniture.

One afternoon, shortly after Archna's death, Kamalbabu was sitting in his armchair looking out into the street. Rama had left a cup of tea for him on a sidetable. He tried to get up from his armchair, but his legs wouldn't do what he wanted them to do. He found himself falling against the table; the cup and saucer, slipping away from him, smashed on the cement floor. The noise alarmed his daughters-in-law. They came running into the room and helped Kamalbabu back into his chair. Dr Mitra was called again. After a short examination, he took Rama and Didi out on to the landing.

'Your father-in-law has had a stroke. He must have complete rest. Can you afford a nurse for him?'

There was no response.

Dr Mitra went on 'Kamalbabu must have some money, surely?'

Didi looked at Rama and then answered, 'Why should Baba have an outsider to nurse him? We can look after him. There's two of us.'

One result of Archna's death was that her daughter renewed her connection with the family. Shima had been brought up as part of this household. She had never lacked love and affection from her grandparents, but she had never felt wanted by her uncles and aunts. From an early age, she had realised that her mother was regarded as a burden, and that her own presence merely made things worse. Her chance came when she was seventeen. She had become friendly with a young man who worked at the corner shop. One morning, leaving a short note for her grandmother, she moved from her grandparents' three-storey house into her new husband's room in the poor part of town. Shima's grandmother was outraged by this action. She felt that Shima had ruined the family's name, and Shima's aunts did everything they could to encourage her anger.

Shima had not gone back to her grandparents' house until the day of her mother's funeral. When her grandmother had died, no one had thought of telling her. Shima had got the news from Bani, her mother's sister. She had sometimes thought of visiting her mother, but her memories of her aunts and uncles were strong enough to keep her away. Her mother's death had broken that barrier, and the news of Kamalbabu's stroke removed all her hesitations. She now became a frequent visitor of the old man's.

Whenever she visited her grandfather, her aunts and uncles

would sit in the room with them. One evening, she decided to raise an issue which had interested her for some time.

'Uncle, what became of mother's old trunk?'

'What do you want to know for?' her aunt replied.

'Maybe it's in the loft,' her uncle suggested.

'I was wondering what happened to mother's jewellery. There were six gold bangles, a pair of earrings and a gold chain.'

'How should we know?' asked her aunt. 'Your grandmother looked after all your mother's things.'

'But surely grandma didn't take them with her when she died?' There was silence. Her aunt left the room and came back with an old trunk. She dragged it into the middle of the floor and threw open the lid. Inside was Archna's wedding sari, the gold thread tarnished and the silk splitting at the folds, and a small basket, decorated with cowrie shells, which Archna had carried as a bride. Apart from that, the trunk was empty. At the sight of these objects, Shima burst into tears.

From his bed, Kamalbabu observed the scene. His stroke had caused a partial paralysis of his face and he could not speak clearly. He opened his mouth to say something but nobody noticed. Shima wiped her eyes and got up to go, but before she left she spoke again.

'You'd better find my mother's jewellery. It can't just disappear. I'll take you to court, if necessary.'

In the days that followed, Kamalbabu remained confined to his bed. Twice a day his daughters-in-law came to his room to serve his meal and give him a wash. Apart from that, he was on his own. There was a feeling of tension in the air. Everybody seemed very busy, and there were whisperings in various parts of the house. Then his older son began to complain about the tenants of the shops on the ground floor.

'The tenants are saying they won't pay their rent unless they get your signature on their rent-books. They won't accept that you're not well enough to sign.'

Didi, who happened to be in the room feeding Kamalbabu, suggested a solution. 'Perhaps Baba could sign a letter of authorisation? The tenants would have to accept that.'

Kamalbabu was still unable to speak. His silence was taken for consent. The next evening Kamalbabu's bed was surrounded by his sons, daughters-in-law and two friends they'd brought in with them. With his weak eyesight and the poor lighting in the room, Kamalbabu could make nothing at all of these papers. His older son leaned towards him.

'Don't worry, Baba. My friends have checked the wording to make sure there's no ambiguity.'

Kamalbabu looked towards them, and the two strangers nodded reassuringly. Rama brought a pen over and held Kamalbabu's unsteady hand to help him sign the documents. His son picked up the two pieces of paper and looked at the signatures.

'There, Baba,' he said. 'There shouldn't be any more problems now.'

While this was happening, Shima had gone to see her Aunt Bani in her small flat on the other side of town. Bani was surprised to see her at the door.

'What has happened? You look ghastly.'

'It's about Ma's jewellery,' Shima began, her voice choking with emotion. 'They say they know nothing about it!'

'They should have handed that over to you after your mother's funeral.'

'Handed it over to me!' said Shima. 'All they've shown me is Ma's empty trunk!'

'Where is her jewellery, then?' Bani asked.

'I don't know.'

'Do you want me to talk to them? It's a pity your grandfather isn't well. If he were able to speak, we could have asked him.'

Shima seemed reassured and Bani persuaded her to sit down and have some tea. When Bani came back from the kitchen, Shima had another question.

'What happens to grandfather's property, when he dies?'

'That depends,' said Bani. 'If he hasn't made a will, then we should all get a share, and you should get your mother's share.'

'And if he has made a will?'

'Then he is quite likely to have left everything to his sons.'

One afternoon, when Rama and Didi were having a long siesta and the servants were busy playing cards under the balcony, Bani and Shima arrived at Kamalbabu's house and found him lying unconscious on the floor of his room. Immediately, the house came to life: the bedclothes were changed, the floor was swept and Dr Mitra was called again.

'We knew something like this would happen!' said Bani. Shima's anger was greater than her aunt's. She shouted, 'Why didn't you hire a nurse? You killed my mother. Now I suppose it's grandpa's turn!'

Her uncle shouted back, 'How dare you come here and insult us!'

'As long as that old man is alive, I'll come as often as I like,' said Shima.

In the middle of this quarrel, Dr Mitra arrived. He examined his patient and then announced that Kamalbabu needed hospital treatment. Kamalbabu was taken to the nearest hospital, and private nurses were hired to look after him twenty-four hours a day. He saw more of his family now than he had ever done before. Shima brought him flowers for his bedside table. Bani kept him supplied with clean towels. His daughters-in-law came to see him regularly so that he wouldn't feel lonely in hospital, after all, the nurses were not his own flesh and blood.

Although Bani and Shima were frequent visitors they weren't able to question Kamalbabu for some time, as the nurse was always there. Their anxiety was more pronounced each time they came to visit him. Eventually there came a moment when the nurse was away from Kamalbabu's bedside. Bani whispered urgently into her father's ear, 'Have you made a will?'

Shima whispered in support, 'Have you signed anything, Grandpa?'

Kamalbabu shook his head. Bani and Shima assumed this could only mean that he hadn't made a will.

After three weeks in hospital, Kamalbabu's flow of visitors began to abate. Bani and Shima made their long journeys across town less frequently. His sons and daughters-in-law made only routine visits. They were, however, very anxious about Kamalbabu's health: they wondered how much longer he would live and how much more of his savings would be needed for his hospital treatment. After a month, Kamalbabu began to show signs of improvement. His facial paralysis had almost disappeared: he could now open his mouth and move his tongue, and he could speak intelligibly again, though slowly.

One day, at the end of an evening visit, when Kamalbabu's youngest son and his wife, Rama, were about to leave the ward, the doctor called them both over.

'You should be able to take your father back home with you within a week. There's nothing more that we can do for him here.' He noticed a worried expression in Rama's eyes and hastened to reassure her. 'Don't worry. He is out of danger now. He should live for a long time.'

Sibani Raychaudhuri

Tiger, Tiger

Smriti was giving the pots and pans a final rub as the sun extinguished itself, dipping gingerly into the ocean. In the jungle clearing surrounding the pond two other women from the village were also there. Smriti's three children were playing on the opposite bank. One of the women sitting next to Smriti thumped clothes on the smooth washing stone, pausing to toss her baby violently up and down to stop it from crying.

Suddenly the raucous cacophony of birds settling down to nest vanished and the shriek of monkeys split the air. Smriti knew what it meant: a tiger was near. Giving her children an urgent shout she started gathering her pots and pans when a fire hot breath fanned down her neck. Then the sharp pain of her skin being punctured and sandpapered. There was no time to shout for help. The tiger began carrying her off, Smriti's body dragging recalcitrantly on the ground.

The two women next to her were galvanised into action. Each held on to one of Smriti's legs, shouting and screaming, frantic with fear. That was when Smriti's eldest daughter, Uma, sprung into action. Taking clear aim at the tiger Uma threw the brass utensils at it. Through the still sentinel jungle rushed reinforcement, a band of honey gatherers on their way home, directly in the getaway path of the tiger.

The tiger, shuddering at changed circumstances roared a ferocious protest that the dinner hunt had turned into a battle for survival, and releasing its hold on Smriti bounded back into the shrubs.

A thick coating of blood stained Smriti's neck, shoulders, back, but one couldn't say where it was coming from. Smriti had fainted. The villagers solemnly carried her to her empty hut. Her husband was away, on a honey-gathering expedition.

'There, you can tell she is alone,' said one of the rescuers, holding out Smriti's hand for those gathered around to see. 'She doesn't wear the red and white shell bangles required by a married woman. Nor the customary vermilion streak on her forehead. Her husband must have gone deep into the jungle.'

Uma silently picked up little red and white pieces from a corner and brought them to the gathered people. 'Mother broke them when Father left for the deep jungle,' she said. 'In accordance with the custom.'

The villagers nod. They know the tradition of preempting widowhood: of a wife taking leave from her husband herself if he is forced into venturing into the deep forest. The risks of the deep forest are deadly, the survival chances small. But when taking that risk is the only way out for the honourable survival of the household the woman freely takes upon herself the trials of a widow, casting away the ritual marriage adornments.

In the Sunderbans, the watery grave of the River Ganges, such customs are common practice. The mangrove forests, with their deformed, gnarled trunks, are exposed at low tide like an army of carefully camouflaged killer squads, symbolic of the lethal dangers that infect the area. The bark of a tree glides noiselessly into the muddy waters. Only the nonchalant flick of the tail gives it away, a crocodile. Far away, on the horizon, the dreaded black shiny triangular forms can be sighted, sharks taunting the fishermen in their rickety boats. Man-eating tigers are another menace . . .

With her husband away, Smriti's welfare was now a common responsibility. A makeshift stretcher was quickly organised and a silent procession armed with spears, rods and burning torches made its way to the water's edge. A convoy of four boats took Smriti and the villagers to the only hospital in the area: in Canning, three hours away. The night was peaceful. The moon painted the water and the forests with silver shine and only the slurping of the oars as they put away the distance to Canning broke the silence.

The hospital was open. Just about. Dust and flaking paint

embraced carelessly on the floor. The night clerk lay on his wooden desk, having perfected the art of sleeping and shaking his legs violently to keep the mosquitoes at bay. Smriti was admitted – the villagers put her stretcher down in an empty room. But there were no doctors to attend. Nor any medically trained personnel present. A message had to be sent to the doctor's home.

'He'll be here soon,' reassured the hospital clerk. 'Can't be a question of many hours. The only problem is if he is away in Calcutta. That'll take a couple of days.'

He shouted and a sleepy-eyed youngster with tousled hair appeared.

'Take this note to the Daktarbabu's house,' the clerk commanded, rubbing the responsibility and note off his hands.

The doctor didn't appear for several hours. One of the villagers organised tea. Sitting around in a small circle near Smriti, they took small sips of tea from the earthen pots to make it last longer. Uttam, one of Smriti's neighbours, went to ask the clerk how long it would take.

'How come so many people get bitten by tigers?' the clerk asked Uttam. 'I've just come a month and this is the third time a person has been mauled by a tiger. The other two cases died.'

Uttam nodded his head knowingly. 'It's the wretched Tiger Project,' he said.

'Tiger Project?' repeated the clerk. 'I'm asking you why is it that so many villagers are mauled by tigers. How can Tiger Project – a project for protecting tigers – cause that?'

Uttam looked at the clerk disbelieving. 'You don't know about that?' Uttam asked incredulously.

'I am a city person, just transferred to this dump against my will. Anyway I don't really believe there is a connection,' the clerk answered, embarrassed and defensive.

'The Tiger Project puts our traditional fishing grounds out of bounds. We aren't allowed to gather honey in the more accessible parts of the forest. Not even allowed to use the less dangerous waterways on our way to the ocean. We'd be disturbing the tigers, the game warden insists,' said Uttam bitterly.

'That has been the cause of our troubles, Smriti's troubles,' said the old woman who had come along to comfort Smriti. 'Her husband has had to give up fishing ever since the area has been declared a wildlife reserve for tigers. Now fishermen have to gather honey for a living in the inner reaches of the jungle. Her father-in-law was carried off by a tiger only a year ago, and now this . . .'

'The government doesn't care more for tigers than people,' said Uttam smoothly. 'It's just that the government was given money to set up this tiger project from abroad. Money which they wouldn't normally have had. And important people from Delhi and abroad are connected with it. How can ordinary people expect to compete? It's better to be a tiger,' Uttam added bitterly.

Loud voices pierce the conversation. A man of obvious authority enters the room. It is the doctor. He walks over to see Smriti and then starts organising things to clean and bandage her. He begins to hum quietly to himself as he prepares all the necessary equipment but stops when he unlocks his medicine cupboard. There are neat little stacks of blue and white boxes filling up half the cupboard but not much else. He turns around, surveying the motley group of villagers around him and asks one of them to come to him. Uttam does.

'Take the first train out to Calcutta and go to the PG hospital. They will give you some medicines to bring back,' the doctor orders.

'But why?' asks Uttam. 'Isn't what you need here? What about all these boxes filling the medicine cupboard?'

'These . . .' says the doctor in an embarrassed, blustering manner, 'are for injured tigers.'

Kanta Talukdar

Right of Way

'A divorced woman with two children! It's absurd! The boy can't be allowed to ruin his life.'

'But if he says he loves the girl?'

'Huh, she's not a girl, she's a woman with two children. And in any case, Daya, what do you know about love since you never married?'

Aunt Daya is silent. Elder sisters may only be contradicted with deference and in this instance a suitable reply calls for reflection.

'Love indeed!' continues Aunt Pushpa. 'What about his love for us? What sort of impression will it create? We'll become a laughing stock. The child doesn't understand.'

The car, turning into a narrow lane, blows up a cloud of dust.

'At thirty-three, you could hardly call him a child.' Aunt Daya is meek.

Aunt Pushpa in reply presses down on the accelerator. The road bends and, as we screech round it, revealed before us is a cow sitting comfortably blocking our path.

'Look out sister!' cries Aunt Daya.

'I can see! I can see!' snaps Aunt Pushpa as she honks loudly to a halt. The cow stays in its place, nonplussed and unperturbed.

'*Hut, hut, hut!* (Get out of the way)' she calls and honks some more, but the cow does not move.

Aunt Daya leans out of the other window and claps her hands efficiently. They wait for a little while, then Aunt Pushpa starts the car and slowly and threateningly proceeds to drive towards the cow.

'Sister, Sister, what are you doing?' exclaims Aunt Daya.

'You'll see. Now it will get up and move,' replies Aunt Pushpa with assurance, clamping down on the horn at the same time. The cow looks at the driver and then simply turns away. Aunt Pushpa stops short in front of the cow and, leaving the engine on, shouts. But the cow hears nothing. She turns the engine off so that it will hear better, and swears! But the cow just doesn't appear to understand.

Pushpa jumps out of the car and strides towards the cow. She pats it to get it to rise and then tries to push it towards the pavement. Unsuccessful, she stands up in annoyance.

On the back seat is a box of fresh vegetables collected during the early morning visit to the farm – the purpose of this journey. Aunt Daya calmly and efficiently tears off a handful of carrot greens which she hands out of the window to Aunt Pushpa. Pushpa takes the greens with resignation, throws them on the pavement and returns to the driving seat. Sitting down with a definite sigh of exasperation, she waits for the cow to move. The cow sits still. Pushpa hoots.

'No, Sister, don't do that. Wait,' says Aunt Daya with ever-growing efficiency, and taking hold of a bunch of fresh, succulent spinach she alights from the car. Holding the bunch in one hand and a single leaf in the other she approaches the cow and offers the leaf.

'Come, come my lotus-eyed beauty. This is for you. Come now and eat it.' The cow looks placidly at my aunt who attempts a reassuring smile.

'Are you going to feed all our lunch to the wretch?' calls out Aunt Pushpa.

'Quiet, Sister, do you want to be here all day?' returns Aunt Daya. The cow accepts the leaf.

'Good, good, take, take,' soothes Aunt Daya as she slowly moves back towards the pavement, holding up the bunch of spinach temptingly.

'Come, come, come, pearl of the universe, come, come, come. Lotus-eyed beauty, come.'

The cow blinks. We all hold our breath. Will she get up?

'Come, my life, come my love, all for you, come, come,' continues Aunt Daya.

The cow concedes. Slowly, and with great dignity, she rises, and then ambles leisurely to the pavement. She accepts the spinach graciously and then goes and sits down comfortably near the greens.

We drive off. Within a gear-change the discussion is resumed as though it had never been interrupted.

Leena Dhingra

Face

Stroking Azure over Brown,
(Her eyes dazzled by colour)

Patting powder to stay,
(Her blemishes hidden by one coat)

Sucking cheeks in for the blusher – Russet Red,
(Dimpling and hollowing out, for a starved gaunt look)

Curling on mascara – Black,
(Still bars across her vision)

Sliding on lips – Blood Red,
(Shaped to please and glisten, not talk)

Gloss like saliva, the final touch
(Watch his mouth eat her face).

Shazia Sahail

A Visit from Guruji

Kamala was eating her breakfast with her family, and memorising multiplication tables for a test at school, when her grandmother came into the room and announced to everyone, 'Last night I had a dream – I dreamt of Guruji!' Before anybody could say anything, she went on, 'Guruji has called upon us – we must invite him to our house. It will be a blessing for us.'

Kamala's parents, her uncle and aunt, her brothers and sisters and cousins were all momentarily silenced by this proposal. Then her uncle jumped up. 'Absurd! Absurd! How could Guruji's feet touch our doorstep?'

Guruji was almost a god to this family. Grandmother had been an ardent devotee since the sudden death of Grandpa. Grandpa was only forty when he died and Grandma was only thirty-three. Her sister-in-law had decided that she 'needed guidance from above'. That's how Guruji came into Grandma's life.

Since she'd been able to understand things, Kamala had heard so much about Guruji: Grandma had told Kamala and Tinu, her younger brother, the story of Guruji's life. Guruji was not an ordinary man. On the eighth night after his birth, auspicious writings had appeared on a palm-leaf beside his cot. At his first rice-eating ceremony, he had picked up the fountain pen and the holy book, and he had learnt the scriptures by heart by the time he was seven.

As an adult, he had performed many miracles. People sought his blessings for arranging their children's marriages; for speedy recovery from illness; for laying foundations of houses; for job interviews; for winning elections, court-cases, lotteries; for buying a new car. In response, Guruji merely smiled – he closed his eyes, stretched out his right arm, and dropped a small half-dead flower upon the supplicant.

Guruji never stayed in any one place for very long. He had thousands of wealthy devotees scattered all over the world. But Kamala's Grandma was not one of these. Guruji had never set foot in their house. Guruji moved from city to city, from country to country. Guruji was often abroad; Guruji was often in hiding – at these times no one was supposed to know where he was. Once Kamala had looked at the postmark on the postcard he had sent to Grandma. She had been delighted with her discovery: 'Grandma! Grandma! Guruji is in France!' Grandma had quickly covered her ears with her hands. She was angry with Kamala. 'We are not to know such things. It is not his wish!'

When Guruji was at home to his followers, anyone might see him, but they had to get tickets beforehand. The tickets were free, but there was always a long queue. Kamala and Tinu had been taken to one of these open days by their grandmother. A huge red cotton canopy had been set up in the grounds of the house of a local cement-dealer. Guruji was sitting amid satin cushions on Persian carpets piled upon a raised platform. He was dressed in saffron-coloured robes; bouquets of roses were laid before him; garlands of jasmine encircled his neck above layers of gold chains. His attendants sat all about him, wafting ivory fans edged with silk to alleviate the heat. These were the members of the inner-cabinet. They had given over their lives to him – and their wealth. In return, they were allowed to follow him wherever he went.

The enormous crowd that had come to see Guruji was seated in rows. The first few rows were reserved for businessmen who had monopolies. Then came smaller businessmen, barristers, judges, government officials. Then came professionals like doctors, engineers, architects, college principals. Then came the lecturers, schoolteachers, office clerks . . . all the way down to street cleaners and street dwellers.

Kamala and Tinu were squashed among the groups towards the back. They watched people taking up gifts to Guruji, and Guruji redistributing the offerings among his followers, once he'd blessed

151

them. The first few rows received shawls and saris. The people at the back received only a lump of sugar. Grandma was given a silk handkerchief. When they got home, Grandma spread the handkerchief on the shrine in her room under the portrait of Guruji.

Now that Grandma had received Guruji's call in her dream, she had to work hard. First she sent an invitation to Guruji, telling him of her dream. When Guruji unexpectedly accepted, then life became a nightmare for the rest of the family. The household was turned upside down. Grandma had everyone cleaning and sweeping and washing. She kept making and remaking plans for the visit: where Guruji was going to sit; which chair he was going to sit on; who was going to speak to him; who was not going to speak to him . . .

At last the great day came. Guruji was due to arrive at nine o'clock on his way to open a new temple. The family was up and ready at the crack of dawn, dressed in their best clothes. Since it was a weekday, Kamala's father and uncle had had to take time off from work. Kamala and Tinu had decided that they would not go to school. The house was so clean that they had to walk on tiptoe. A chair had been placed in the middle of the front room, with a small piece of carpet on the seat. They had bought flowers and fruit and sweets for Guruji, and they stood waiting in tense silence. Grandma bustled around, adding the final touches: 'Kamala, take down that film-star calendar – Guruji will be annoyed. And don't open your mouth, Tinu, unless he speaks to you first.'

It was almost five past nine – and the sun was getting warmer and warmer – but still there was no sign of Guruji's car. Kamala and Timu listened to every car-engine as it came towards them, and then went past. At quarter past nine, a man in white robes knocked on their door. Grandma ran to open it. It was not Guruji – it was his messenger. He said something to her in a low voice – and the rest of the family looked at each other. 'Is he not coming, then?' was the unspoken question.

The messenger left, and Grandma came back towards them. 'It's his car,' she said. 'It's too big to come down the lane. We will have to go out to see him.'

They packed all their offerings into a basket, and set off down the lane to where Guruji was sitting in the back of a shiny-new, silver-grey car. Grandma was carrying a pitcher of water to wash his feet, but as she got closer she saw he was wearing shoes and socks. They went forward, one by one, to touch his feet, while the messenger put the basket into the boot. In five minutes, everything was over. The car doors were closed, and the big car glided away. The lane was as empty as if Guruji had never been there.

Sibani Raychaudhuri

Buying Romance

Today, I bought a love
A story.
I bought a happy ending.
I bought into a closed world.
I bought a Hero.
I am a Heroine
Always quietly beautiful
Inside and out.
I bought my Hero
And felt safe and secure
For a while.
He was tall, handsome and strong
Very broad-shouldered.
Wealthy and successful, of course.
I bought my quota of happiness
Consolation for the unloved me
Of the real world
On the Dole.

Today, I bought a love
A story.
Everything comes out right
In this dream of Romance.
I am not an addict.
It leaves no hangover.
It contains no calories.
It keeps me quiet
For an hour or so.
Today I bought
Dependence and
Dissatisfaction.

Shazia Sahail

154

War of the Worlds

'You two want to do what you want? Behave as you please?' Mum's voice hard and strained, refusing to shed the tears flooding her eyes. 'If you don't like living here, you can leave. Both of you.' It was like being given ECT. Little shockwaves burned through us. I could see Suki's eyes growing larger and larger, expanding exponentially. Mum had never said anything like this to us before.

She'd never blamed us before, she'd blamed the nurse in the hospital when we were born. 'Twin daughters,' she'd told Mum, bearing one on each arm. 'Aren't they sweet? Sweet on the outside, acid on the inside,' she'd said sing-song. 'Oh, they're going to be terrible. The Terrible Twins!' chuckling away.

'Because your father isn't around any more . . .' Mum still couldn't bring herself to use words like dead . . . 'you think you no longer need to watch your tongue, or have respect for other people. And you never have to come back. Have your freedom.' Scooping up the baby, marching off upstairs.

It wasn't that we'd changed, things had. We'd been wilder than wild even when Dad was alive: running round town like we were urban guerrillas of the Asian kind. No part of town we didn't know, no person we didn't suss out, no action we didn't know about. The town was our battleground. Our Frontline. Dad would rave and rant at us, tell us we were shameless, not fit to live in civilised society and did we know what happened to women like us? Dad wanted us to be accommodating, to fit in, to live like decent people. We know what 'decent' people get up to when they think no one's looking, we argued back, like there seems to be one set of rules people use if they think they're going to be found out and another set if they think they can do whatever they want in safe secrecy. And it's not as if everyone doesn't know what's going on. They're all happy to shut their eyes to it 'cos they don't want to rock the boat and they don't want to grass on anyone else in case they get grassed on themselves.

Mum and Dad copped it from us every time. We were part of them and they were part of us and that's why we could never be soft with them. If we got them to agree with us, just once, it was like the gates were opened for us to take on the whole world.

And now Mum was saying we could leave. Go. Do what we want. Walk out the front door. We both swivelled our heads to look towards it, though of course we couldn't see it from where we were sitting. Suki and I didn't look at each other; we didn't have to. Mum's ultimatum was ticking like a time-bomb in our brains.

Freedom!

We both stood up, went towards the front door and opened it. It was a beautiful summer evening: balmy, cool, fragrant. Real tourist brochure stuff. We stepped out, over the threshold.

'Charlie's having her party tonight,' said Suki.

'Probably be the same old crowd.'

'We should go to London. Thousands of new people there.'

'Millions. And new things to do.'

'Living on our own.'

'Making it in the Metropolis.'

A car drove by and the bloke in it waved to us. We both waved back, our arms like enthusiastic windscreen wipers. We could hear him reversing his car further up the road, the gravel crunching under his tyres. The blokes loved doing that. Made them feel like Action Man come alive. His engine noise zoomed towards us and then stopped as the car came to a body-shaking, gravel-crunching stop outside our gate.

'You gonna go?' asked Suki.

'I did him last time. He won't know the difference.'

She sauntered off towards him and I sat peeling grass blades, till a pile of curled green strips lay at my feet.

Their voices rose and fell, scraps of sentences floated back to me, followed by occasional riffs of laughter; Suki was leading him on, making him think he had a chance. He didn't of course. He was too ordinary. His flash car and trendy clothes couldn't make up for the mediocre stuff in his brain. I was surprised he hadn't heard of us, hadn't been warned off going near the terrible twins. We had a whole pack of enemies in town, not least among them, the blokes who'd sworn they loved us madly and couldn't live without us. Until we put our reject stamp on them.

Suki and I always compared notes and it was always the same old story: unimaginative, unintelligent. Men who thought they were God's special gift to Asian women. The white blokes wanted to liberate us from our 'primitive' traditions and customs; the Asian blokes thought weren't we lucky to be loved by them in spite of our dubious reputations and bad style of life. Nothing guaranteed to make us run faster and further than blokes imagining themselves to be 'In Love' with us. We'd seen enough of the after-effects of 'In Love' to make us avoid it like the proverbial plague.

First there was Janet, whose bloke had been 'In Love' with her, had chased her for months till she'd finally come round, as they say; come to her senses, he'd said. And Paul had been ever so romantic, insisting on a church wedding, white dress, whisking her off to a grand honeymoon. Janet don't talk about Love no more though – bit difficult when half your teeth been knocked out, and all the other bits of your body knocked in.

Then there was our cousin, Jeeta. Got to be fair, he hadn't said he loved Kulwinder. Just that he forgot to tell her that he'd promised his love to the *gori* next door; just that he didn't have the guts to tell his mother, either, as she busily went about arranging his marriage to Kulwinder. Kulwinder who was sweet, obedient and modest, the perfect Indian girl, the perfect Indian bride.

'Being perfect didn't stop her getting messed up, did it?' said Suki in one of her sarky moods.

Kulwinder did her best. We know she tried hard, but she was too innocent, too simple for his tactics, and he knew she didn't know how to fight back. He wanted to drive her away by driving her to a nervous breakdown; that much she sussed out and flew the nest before the rot could set in.

Suki and I couldn't believe it. The whole family, even our Mum and Dad, sided with him: they said she should have tried harder, been more patient, understanding. Marriage wasn't the easy option the West made it out to be. It had to be worked at, sacrifices and compromises made. 'Sita-Savitri doesn't live here any more, don't you know?' I said. Wasted my inter-cultural mythical allusions, didn't I, 'cos they all turned round and looked as blank as blank at me.

Suki and I wanted to make Halal meat out of Jeeta and serve him up to Kulwinder on a platter, but she wouldn't have none of it. She was too good an Indian girl to get mixed up in revenge and justice, and anyway her father had to think of her future. He'd have to start looking for another marriage for her. She mustn't jeopardise her chances.

Then there was the time we brought Shanti and her baby home.

'They've been thrown out of their home, Mum, and an English woman was trying to help her, but you know how none of these *goras* can speak Punjabi . . .'

'Illiterate lot,' added Suki, interrupting my grand speech. Mum took her in and Mum and Mum's friends all gathered round to help. They brought clothes for Shanti and the baby, they cooked food for them, they condoled, they consoled, they commiserated and then stood back as Shanti and baby went back to her horrible husband. We couldn't understand it and attacked Mum for driving her back.

'Shanti thought it over and made her own choice,' said Mum.

'Some choice,' muttered Suki.

'That's all some women get.'

'It's wrong.'

'Yes,' replied Mum, seeming to agree with us for once, 'but it won't be for long, will it? You two are going to change the world, aren't you?' She could be dead sarcastic, our mum.

We couldn't let it go, could we? We decided on direct action: decided to get them at the Gurudwara. Anyone could get up and speak. The men did it all the time, giving long lectures on righteous living and long-winded explanations of God's thoughts and intentions; they all talked like they had a hot line to the heavens. We'd made sure we were dressed proper and started off by reading a verse from Suki's *Gotka* (no, she hadn't got religion, just thought it was 'bootiful' poetic stuff. Mum and Dad would get ever so pleased when they saw her reading it – thinking that the light of goodness had finally touched their wayward daughter). I've done a lot of things in my (short) life, but getting up there in front of all them Sunday-come-to-worship-people was the toughest. It started off all sweet and nice, the mothers and grandmothers smiling at us, whispering among themselves about how nice it was to see us young women taking part. I sneaked a glance at Dad. Shouldn't have. His eyes were sending out laser beams of anger. He knew we were up to something.

Finishing the verse, we started in on our talk, speaking our best Punjabi and careful not to let our dupattas slip off our heads. We began by saying that there was much suffering in our community and that we, as the Gurudwara, should organise to do something about it. For instance there should be a fund for women who have to leave home because they are being beaten or ill-treated; the Gurudwara should arrange accommodation as well as helping them with education and training and make sure they weren't outcast by the rest of the community. Rather the Gurudwara should praise them for having the courage to liberate themselves from cruelty, just as India had liberated herself from the cruelty of the Raj (rather a neat touch, I thought: the linking of the personal to the political, the micro to the macro). It was as if the windows had banged open and let in a hot strong wind; a susurration of whispers eddied to and fro.

They didn't know we'd only given them the hors d'oeuvre. We then suggested that the problem should be tackled at the root: men were not going to have respect for women unless they had respect for women's work; therefore the boys should be taught cooking, cleaning, babycare, etc. The men sniggered, some laughed out loud.

'Men who beat or mistreat their wives should be heavily fined by the Gurudwara, and if they persist should be cast out from our society. And if they've taken a dowry they should be made to return it, in double. Blokes who make girls pregnant and then leave them in the lurch should never be allowed to have an arranged marriage . . .' We had to stop 'cos Pati's dad, Harcharan Singh, stood up and launched into an attack on us. We were really disgusted! That man spent more money on his drinking and smoking than he did on his family, and still wanted them to be grateful for whatever scraps he threw their way. This man was now standing up and accusing us of being corrupt and dangerous; others were nodding their heads in agreement.

'Are you saying these things don't happen?' we asked, all innocent like.

I don't think he even heard, just carried on with his diatribe against 'children who don't know their place and women who have no respect for tradition and custom.' Others couldn't wait and interrupted until there were several voices all speaking at once. One voice strained above the others and accused us of bringing dirt and filth into the house of God and getting a bit carried away he let slip a couple of nasty words. Mistake, because Mrs Gill, who was a Moral Majority in her own right, got up immediately and rounded on him like a 40-ton truck. Adjusting her dupatta like a gunslinger adjusting his holster, she told him it was his rotten tongue defiling the house of God and why couldn't the men sit quiet and let the girls finish what they were saying.

'We should listen to our young sometimes,' she said. 'We may learn something.' She gave us the all-clear nod and sat back down among the women.

This was the crunch, the lunge for the jugular vein, and as I formed the words and reached for the microphone I found my voice, Suki's voice, reaching out, spreading across the hall: 'It's no good coming to the Gurudwara once a week to show how clean and pure you are, it doesn't hide all the sordid, underhand things that have been happening all week. The Gurudwara isn't the disinfectant that kills 99 per cent of all germs. It should be treated with more respect. In turn we who are the Gurudwara should get tough on those men who harass us women, whistle at us, touch us up, attempt to force us into their cars . . . Some of them are sitting right here and they know who they are.' Like a storm among the trees angry, aggrieved whispers were rustling around the men . . . 'What about the man who's started a prostitution racket? He's here. And

160

those who can't tell the difference between their daughters and their wives . . .' The place exploded, most rising to their feet, some raising their fists to us, others moving forward, pushing through towards us.

Dad had saved us. Defused the danger. The crowd had parted to let him through.

'I suppose we'll have to call him Moses after this,' whispered Suki. He stopped by us and turned round to face the others.

'It's late. I'm going to take my daughters home. But we can't go without having Prasad.' Picking up the covered bowl of warm Prasad Dad served us each with a round ball of the gorgeous delicious sweet, whispering to us to meet him by the car. He turned round and started serving those nearest to us. Prasad is God's food and you're not supposed to refuse it. You should be glad it's offered to you.

'D-a-d is O-u-r C-h-a-m-p-i-o-n.' All the way home we wanted to chant 'D-a-d is O-u-r C-h-a-m-p-i-o-n,' like the football fans do, but he was in a foul mood so we shut up and kept quiet.

'We think what you did was really brave,' said Preeti during the dinner break at school.

'Yeah. Those things really needed to be said,' added Bhupinder, her short pigtails swishing round her face; she never had been able to grow her hair below shoulder length, despite all the creams and lotions she poured on to it.

'So why didn't you say anything?' asked Suki. 'We could have used some help.'

'You kidding? Mum would have come down on me like Two Tons of Bricks.'

'Gutless goons always want other people to do their fighting for them,' I said, hoping it sounded as sarky as I felt.

'No one asked you to do it,' put in Preeti, coming to her best friend's aid. 'Anyway you two fancy yourselves as Revolutionaries.'

'Freedom Fighters,' added stupid Bhupinder with a stupid giggle. 'We wouldn't want to take your glory from you.'

'And not everyone's got liberal parents like yours.' Poison Preeti again.

161

Liberal parents! That sure was history, what with Mum as good as throwing us out of the house! Suki was trying to say goodbye to the thing at the gate, his arms stretching out to hold her back, impress her with his burning passion. She moved back towards him once, twice, and I thought, this is silly, why's she wasting her time on him when we've got to talk and make decisions?

'You were right. He's a dead loss.' Her skirt swished by me as she sat down.

'There must be some who aren't.'

'We'll have to go looking for them, won't we?'

'Mum doesn't want us here if we don't change.'

'You want to leave?' Suki turned round to look at me, face on, full frontal.

'I'm not scared of leaving.'

'Not the point.'

'There's always white people and white society . . .?' My voice sounded as if posing a maths problem.

'They'll want us to change to their ways . . .' Suki came back as sharp as a knife.

Silence between the two of us. For a change! I picked up the shredded bits of grass and shifted them through my fingers. 'Not much choice, is there? I guess it's a case of Here to Stay–Here to Fight.'

Suki giggled. 'Old slogans never die, eh?'

I had an idea. I thought it was brilliant. 'Let's go to Patel's.' Suki caught on as I knew she would. 'And see if he's got any mangoes for Mum? Right.'

We closed the gate very carefully behind us, in case Mum heard and wondered.

Ravinder Randhawa

Notes on the Contributors

Rukhsana Ahmad taught English language and literature at the University of Karachi, Pakistan, before coming to live in the United Kingdom in 1973. She has worked as a freelance journalist and has written several plays for Tara Arts Company, the most recent of which is *Black Shalwar*. She is currently working on a play commissioned by the feminist theatre group Monstrous Regiment.

Leena Dhingra is a freelance writer who came to Europe from India after Partition in 1947. She has worked as a film technician, a publicity officer, and a teacher. She was a contributor to *Watchers and Seekers* (The Women's Press, 1987) and has just completed her first novel *Amritvela* (The Women's Press, 1988). She is currently working on a social/family history about the Punjab at the turn of the century. She lives in London with her daughter.

Rahila Gupta is a journalist who received her BA in English and French at the University of Bombay, India, and did an M. Phil in drama at the Polytechnic of Central London. She has edited *Shakti* magazine, and has been active in the women's movement and various campaigns on immigration/deportation, race issues and the Police Bill. She is on the editorial collective of *Outwrite* magazine, and has contributed to *Charting the Journey* (Sheba Press, 1988).

Ravinder Randhawa is a writer who has contributed to the anthology *A Girl's Best Friend* (The Women's Press, 1987) and *More to Life than Mr Right* (Piccadilly Press, 1985). Her first novel, *A Wicked Old Woman*, was published by The Women's Press in 1987, and she is

163

currently working on her second.

Sibani Raychaudhuri is a teacher who was born and brought up in Calcutta. Her English translations of Bengali poetry have appeared in *The Times Literary Supplement* and the *London Magazine*. She has written for *Spare Rib* and *Artrage*, and has been active in promoting South-Asian literature through the South-Asian Literature Society. She has recently published *Intabiler Puntmi*, a collection of tales for Bengali speakers. She is also editing an anthology of poetry written in Bengali by Bengali women living in Britain.

Shazia Sahail received her BA in cultural studies at North-East London Polytechnic. She has worked as a youth leader for Asian girls, and was a librarian and information worker at the Feminist Library in London; she is currently working as a housing officer. She has written for *Artrage*, and has given readings at various venues in London.

Meera Syal obtained a degree in English and Drama at Manchester University and devised a one-woman show, *One of Us*, with Jacqui Shapiro – a comedy drama about an Indian girl from Birmingham who runs away from home because she wants to be an actress. Since joining The Asian Women Writers' Workshop, she has written another one-act woman show, *The Leather Mongoose*, for Channel Four, and has just completed her first film script for the BBC. She will shortly be starting on a play commissioned for the Royal Court Theatre in London.

Kanta Talukdar is a freelance writer and journalist who has been a longtime correspondent for several Indian magazines and newspapers. She contributed a short story to *A Girl's Best Friend* (The Women's Press, 1987), has written a book on London entitled *London and its History* (I. P. Verlagessellschaft, 1987), and her first full-length play will be performed by the Hounslow Arts Centre in 1988. One of her main interests is development in India, and she has founded several organisations in this field in her native India. She is currently writing a novel.

Leena Dhingra
Amritvela

'The non-stop flight to New Delhi is half-way. But
only my watch informs me of that. Through the
window we appear quite immobile, suspended over
a vast expanse of curdling clouds. If, as I have often
said, I feel myself suspended between two cultures,
then this is where I belong, the half-way mark.'

Meera's return to her family home in India after years of
living in England is a dismaying jumble of comfort and
frustration, familiarity and bewilderment. Even the simple
chore of posting a parcel becomes a complex ritual that has
to be learnt, memorised and performed in the time-
honoured *Indian* way. She finds herself a child again to her
protective old aunts, an innocent to her sophisticated
cousins. As a woman between two cultures, can she ever
hope to be to be at home in her own country again?

Leena Dhingra is a startling new talent and already a stylist
of rare sensitivity and distinction.

Fiction   £3.95
ISBN: 0 7043 4113 1

Sharan-Jeet Shan
In My Own Name
An Autobiography

From childhood, Sharan-Jeet had a mind of her own. She chafed
against the restrictions of her status as a girl in the Punjab, subject
to the authority now of her father, in the future of a husband. So
she set out to train as a doctor, but when she fell in love with a
Muslim the full wrath of her Sikh family descended upon her. She
was taken out of medical school, locked up, beaten, and eventually
forced into an arranged marriage...

Even when her marriage carried her to a strange country, she
didn't give up. The story of how she struggled to assert her own
autonomy and establish a home of her own is one of extraordinary
courage, faith and determination.

Autobiography/Black and Third World Women's Studies   £3.95
ISBN: 0 7043 3974 9

Kali for Women (editors)
Truth Tales
Stories by Indian Women

Shubha the doctor, Shakun the dollmaker, Jashoda the
wetnurse, and Tiny's Granny, the polished and accomplished
beggar 'famed for her sleight of hand', are just a few of the
many memorable women to be encountered in these assured
and skilful stories.

Here at last is a chance to explore India's *popular* literary
tradition – a flourishing tradition which includes a wealth of
writing by women and which has hitherto been unavailable in
Britain. Translated from Bengali, Urdu, Hindi, Marathi, Gujarati
and Tamil, these stories offer a rich mosaic of Indian life (town
and country life, young people and old, wealth and poverty)
and represent some of the most dynamic trends in Indian
writing today.

Fiction: £3.95
ISBN: 0 7043 4001 1
Hardcover £8.95
ISBN 0 7043 5000 9

Ravinder Randhawa
A Wicked Old Woman

Stick-leg-shuffle-leg-shuffle: decked out with NHS specs and
Oxfam coat, Kulwant masquerades behind her old woman's
disguise, taking life or leaving it as she feels inclined, seeking new
adventures or venturing back into her past.

Divorced from her husband, disapproved of by her sons,
mistrusted by their wives, Kuli makes real contact through a
jigsaw of meetings in the present: with Bahadur the Punjabi punk
who dusts her down after a carefully calculated fall, with
Caroline, her gregarious friend from school days, who watched
over her dizzy romance with 'Michael the archangel', with Maya
the myopic who can't see beyond her weeping heart, and with
Shanti who won't see, whose eyes will remain closed till her
runaway daughter returns to the fold.

A sharply observed first novel set in an Asian community in a
British city – a witty and confident piece of work from a talented
new writer.

Fiction   £4.95
ISBN: 0 7043 4078 X
Hardback   £12.95
ISBN: 0 7043 5032 7

The Women's Press is a feminist publishing house. We aim to publish a wide range of lively, provocative books by women, chiefly in the areas of fiction, literary and art history, physical and mental health and politics.

To receive our complete list of titles, send a large stamped addressed envelope. We can supply books direct to readers. Orders must be pre-paid in £ sterling with 60p added per title for postage and packing (70p overseas). We do, however, prefer you to support our efforts to have our books available in all bookshops.

The Women's Press, 34 Great Sutton Street, London EC1V 0DX